MW01051705

SUCCESSFUL LEADERSHIP TODAY

This book is dedicated to

Wayne, Kenneth,

and

The University of Maryland.

**"There is no security
on this earth.
Only *OPPORTUNITY.*"
GENERAL DOUGLAS MACARTHUR**

SUCCESSFUL

LEADERSHIP

TODAY

Professional Management Spectrum, Inc.

Publisher

Pensacola, Florida

SUCCESSFUL LEADERSHIP TODAY

This book was written and designed to give the reader an easy, effective reference to leadership principles and concepts.

The contents of this book should be digested over time to fully comprehend the contents. For best results, read only a limited number of pages at a time. Read a few new pages every day. Then, put what you have read into practice.

Refer back to this book at regular intervals and on a continuing basis.

To become a successful leader today, do not simply read this book--DO IT, LIVE IT.

1

BUILD

SELF CONFIDENCE

IN OTHERS

—

A *GOOD* leader inspires others with his or her own confidence; a *GREAT* leader inspires them with confidence in themselves.

Take the time to thank and congratulate people for a job well done. The more times people receive positive feedback the more self-confident they become. At the same time, a "chewing out" for a minor imperfection detracts from self confidence.

Building self-confidence in others and helping them overcome obstacles and fear increases their value to themselves and to your team. Do not put people in a job over their head. *Be a cheerleader* and help others build their self confidence.

> **"Hidden talent
> counts for nothing."
> NERO**

2

OBSERVE

SUCCESSFUL

PEOPLE

Observe the traits and habits of successful people around you. Incorporate their strong points into your leadership and management style.

Be particularly watchful of people who have more experience than you. Notice how individual situations are handled. Do not miss the small points.

INTEGRITY

Firm adherence to a code of
moral artistic values.

Soundness, adherence to moral
principal and character.

Incorrupt. Honest.

3

REPEAT

INFORMATION &

INSTRUCTIONS

Your important information and instructions should be repeated and restated. At the end of a day at work the average person has correctly retained only about 25 percent of the verbal input received. The other 75 percent was misunderstood or forgotten. Ask people to repeat important information back to you.

The goals or objectives of difficult or lengthy projects should be restated from time to time.

> **Discover yourself first. Everything else will follow.**

4

HAVE NO

UNENFORCED

RULES

There should be no unenforced rules. Rules and regulations that are not enforced in letter and spirit are corrosive and undermine the effectiveness of all rules and regulations. Work to get the unenforceable rules eliminated and to enforce the rules that are in effect.

Most people do not violate major rules and regulations. Be alert for minor violations. Several people violating minor rules could become a major problem.

> **Know exactly where you are going before you start leading others.**

5

PROVIDE GUIDELINES

FOR

JOB COMPLETION

When you give someone a task to complete, provide guidelines on the time requirement. Then, have that person inform you when the task is completed.

If you have to keep checking back with people on every task you assign, you may become bogged down in petty details.

Set realistic completion times. If you allow too little time, shortcuts may be taken and the job may not be top quality. If you allow too much time, the job may be stretched out to meet your deadline. In the latter case, you have lost efficiency.

> "Never tell people HOW to do things. Tell them WHAT to do and they will surprise you with their ingenuity."
> GENERAL GEORGE S. PATTON

6

HAVE

MUTUAL TRUST

IN OTHERS

You should assume that all persons with whom you conduct business are basically honest and are doing their best. This should hold true until you have evidence to the contrary on an individual basis.

You would not want someone working with you for the first time to automatically distrust you. If you want to have the trust of others, give them your trust first.

> Lack of enthusiasm
> is a
> self-destructive
> weakness.

7

REQUEST,

DON'T

DEMAND

———

Do not **DEMAND** something from someone when you only have to **REQUEST** it. It is a better leadership style to ask that something be done instead of always ordering or demanding that it be done. Phrase requests in the following manner:

"Would you ..."
"Could you ..."
"How about ..."
"Can you..."
"Let's get started on ..."
"We need to ..."
Etc.

Demand only when asking does not work. Treat others as you wish to be treated.

Patience builds character.

8

LEADERSHIP

RESPONSIBILITY

PRIORITIES

1ST RESPONSIBILITY - A leader's *FIRST* responsibility is to keep all subordinates gainfully employed in carrying out the goals and objectives of the organization.

2ND RESPONSIBILITY - The *SECOND* responsibility is for the leader to be usefully employed in completing those goals and objectives.

Do not focus too much on the first responsibility. In this case, you are busy but your subordinates are either not working, or they are not working in the correct areas. Stay on top of your subordinate's work *BEFORE* you start on your personal work.

9

PROVIDE

INCENTIVE

People need a reason to do something, an incentive. A leader's job is to provide that incentive.

Remember, a reward is a good incentive; A "*threat*" is not a good incentive.

Determine what motivates each individual. Then, find an incentive that will motivate each individual or group.

Public recognition is a good incentive. A personal "pat on the back" for a job well done is a good incentive.

Remember that individuals have different things that motivate them. Tailor the incentive to get the motivation you need.

> **Find a meaningful**
> **way to say**
> **"*thank you*"**
> **when it is deserved.**

10

PLAN

FOR

TOMORROW

———

Take a couple quiet minutes at the end of each work day to make a written list of the most important things that need to be worked on the next work day. If you cannot do this at work, do it at home.

The next day, keep that list with you and make sure the jobs are completed. Don't be diverted by less important matters.

If you take this approach to your job each day you should notice your organization becoming more focused on the important matters and more efficient.

> **Want a valuable asset? Tell someone they are.**

11

A SINCERE

"THANK YOU"

IS APPRECIATED

When was the last time someone said "*thank you*" to you and really meant it? Whenever it was, you probably got a real good feeling about yourself, and the person who thanked you. When someone does something meaningful for you, or when someone goes out of their way for you, give them a personal "thank you."

Your personal "thank you" shows appreciation and gratitude. These two little words can spread goodwill and teamwork faster than almost any other collection of words.

> **Keep the workplace clean, neat and orderly. It sets the stage for the kind of work you expect.**

12

IF YOU CAN'T

CONTROL IT,

FORGET IT

Just like the weather, some things are out of your control. Don't be too concerned about things you cannot control. To do so takes your focus off things you can, and should, be controlling.

"Nothing is more difficult, and therefore more precious, than to be able to decide."
NAPOLEON

13

PERSONAL

GOAL

RE-EVALUATION

Re-evaluate yourself and your overall career goals from time to time. "Are the goals I set for myself 2-3 years ago still valid? Did I set my goals too low or too high? Have I reached a point in my career where I need to set and achieve other goals?" You are not the person today you were 2-3 years ago.

You should make long-term career goals of at least five years into the future. Break the 5-year plan down into individual prioritized, chronological steps, or goals. Then, make a short-range goal of completing that first long-range goal. Reevaluate your goals periodically to see if they are realistic and remain valid.

> Get someone to organize an after-work social event to break up the day-in, day-out work routine.

14

PRAISE IN PUBLIC

CONDEMN

IN PRIVATE

———

When someone does commendable work they deserve praise. This praise should be demonstrated in a public setting, in front of co-workers, so ·that the individual receives recognition. Praising in public reinforces high standards being met, recognizes good work, and helps build morale. Praising in private does not have the same effect.

Condemning in public is something like a public slap in the face. This also "airs dirty laundry" in front of others. *DO NOT* condemn others in public.

> **Don't be satisfied with satisfactory.**

15

RINGING

OFFICE

PHONE

Ensure the phone in your office, or on your desk, is answered within 2-3 rings. A phone ringing excessively shows lack of attention and professionalism. In addition, it might be your boss calling.

You should have a standard policy throughout your organization to have telephones answered in a timely and professional manner.

Offering incentives is
incentive
in and of itself.

16

TAKE

PERSONAL

INITIATIVE

Adopt the habit of taking the initiative on projects and tasking. Ask for work. Job variety and diversity help you grow professionally and sets a good example for your subordinates.

One of the most important aspects of a leader is *initiative*. In fact, that is one definition of a leader. No one gets ahead in today's world without taking some initiative. Be willing to do more than "just get by."

COURAGE

Quality of mind or spirit that
allows one to face difficulty.

Mental or moral spirit.

Quality of spirit and conduct.

Mettle. Spirit. Resolution. Tenacity.

17

KEEP

PAPERWORK

TO A MINIMUM

Do not generate paperwork unless it is absolutely necessary. Paperwork has a way of cluttering up desks and work schedules. Managing and accounting for paperwork takes others away from actual work accomplishment.

If you initiate only one memorandum, it has to be accounted for and delivered to the addressee. The addressee may have to respond with another memo and then place both memos in a file or folder. Soon, this becomes an endless cycle of back-and-forth paperwork.

Paperwork should be generated only to serve as some kind of official record. Make personal contact or use the telephone whenever possible to avoid extra paperwork.

> **No one is offended by writing that is easy to understand.**

18

MAKE

THINGS

HAPPEN

___

As a leader or manager you must *MAKE THINGS HAPPEN* to be successful. Do not stand around waiting for someone else to do something. Become involved. Get things going. Taking the lead *is* leadership..

Keep yourself and your people busy making things happen. Do not be misled into thinking that *activity* alone is sufficient. You must determine that the activity is actually producing results.

> "Courage is
> grace
> under pressure."
> ERNEST HEMMINGWAY

19

PROVIDE

COUNSELING

Provide a helpful, private forum to discuss the professional performance, development and growth of subordinates. One-on-one counseling can be immensely beneficial to subordinates and to the organization.

Start counseling sessions on a positive note, pointing out strong areas and successes. Ask the individual to comment *first* in areas where he or she might see room for improved performance. Say something like, "How would you rate your performance in (area)?" Or, "How are you doing in (area)?" Offer ideas and suggestions for possible improvement. End the counseling session on a positive, up-beat note.

Keep abreast of
current world events.

20

MAINTAIN

A

PHONE LIST

Keep an up-to-date phone number listing of people whom you may wish to contact. The list should include superiors, subordinates, other organizations (with names) of interest, and emergency offices and personnel.

Keep a copy at work, at home, and either on your person or in your car. Above all, keep the list up to date.

> **Recognize
> and reward
> creativity and
> resourcefulness**

21

OTHERS ARE NOT

AGAINST YOU

Do not start to feel that you are alone in some of your endeavors. *REMEMBER, OTHERS ARE NOT AGAINST YOU, THEY ARE SIMPLY FOR THEMSELVES.*

If you need the help of other people, it is your job to find a way to make others feel that they have a stake in the outcome of a particular task or project. They need an incentive.

Success is 1% inspiration and 99% perspiration.

22

MAKE

IMMEDIATE CHANGES

IF NECESSARY

When you take over an organization that has not been performing well, make changes immediately.   That is, immediately after you diagnose the problems and come up with solutions.

People expect some changes when a new person takes over the helm.   If you wait too long, they will not expect the changes and they will assume the operating routine should continue as it has in the past.

> "Before everything else,
> getting ready
> is the
> secret of success."
> HENRY FORD

23

MOTIVATING

INCENTIVES

Remember, the incentives that drive you may not be the same incentives that drive the next person. Know what motivates those around you. Some motivating incentives are:

1) SENSE OF BELONGING

2) SENSE OF RESPECT

3) SENSE OF RECOGNITION

4) SENSE OF ACCOMPLISHMENT/ACHIEVEMENT

5) ADVANCEMENT/PROMOTION

6) INCREASED RESPONSIBILITY/AUTHORITY

The list could go on and the exact priority will vary with each individual.

Trust, but verify.

24

RESPECT

IS

EARNED

See to it *EACH DAY* that the people working for you have at least one good reason to respect you. This can be in almost any form: leadership, character, courage, work ethics, etc.

You must earn respect; you cannot demand it. At the same time, show others they have earned your respect.

Always show proper respect toward those above you. This sets the stage for the people working for you to have respect for you.

> **Develop a sense of curiosity about everything going on around you.**

25

SUPPORT

YOUR

PEOPLE

Support and help your people.   If someone needs something, see that he or she gets it.   If your people need some professional or personal assistance, support them. See that they get the assistance they need.

Stand up for your people when necessary.   Go out of your way to provide the help and support they need.   Support your people and they will support you.

"The wise are instructed by reason;
ordinary minds by experience;
the stupid, by necessity;
and brutes by instinct."
CICERO

26

GET

THE INFORMATION

YOU SEEK

Always get the information you seek from someone. If it was not important, you would not be asking for it.

Do not accept generalities. Do not accept half-answers. If you need specific information, don't be satisfied until you get specific information.

If someone should know the information you are looking for but does not, ask them to do research. Have others do most research work. They need to learn and you do not have the time to research everything.

> A leader inspires
> and motivates
> people toward a
> common purpose.

27

DON'T BE AFRAID

TO ASK

FOR ASSISTANCE

———

If you find you need outside help or assistance to successfully complete tasks or projects, ask for it. Do not wait until a deadline has been missed. Then it's too late. Be timely in your request for assistance.

First, ask co-workers or peers for assistance. If that does not work, ask your superior. No deadlines should be missed, or projects not completed, because you are reluctant to ask for assistance. Everyone needs help and assistance from time to time. Do not always try to do everything by yourself.

> "No matter what may be the
> ability of the officer, if he
> loses the confidence of
> his troops, disaster must
> sooner or later ensue."
> GENERAL ROBERT E. LEE

28

DO NOT

ALLOW

COMPLACENCY

Set high standards and do not allow complacency to seep into your organization. The successful conclusion of one job or task should be a stepping stone to the next assignment. Do not allow yourself or others to rest on past accomplishments. You build on success; you do not rest on it.

When one goal is met, set another one, and then another one. Keep moving ahead.

Watch the action and listen to the words of others. Worry when you hear words like, "That should be good enough." Be on the lookout for this type of complacency. Focus on and stress improvement. Maintaining the status quo should not be good enough for you or your people.

> **Need a vision for the future?**
> **Mentally place yourself there**
> **and look around.**

29

SUPPORT

YOUR

SUPERIORS

Support *ALL* your superiors in public. Ask them questions in private. Showing distrust or resentment toward your superiors in public is contagious. Soon, your people will be doing it to you.

It is counterproductive not to show public support to your superiors.

Frequent verbal support from seniors is a great motivator.

30

MAKE

A GOOD

FIRST IMPRESSION

You never get a second chance to make a first impression. Your dress, attitude and mannerism will make an immediate impression on others.

Go out of your way to make a good first impression. This is especially true when meeting your boss or other professional people. Maintain a positive attitude and outlook throughout these first encounters.

Make sure all of your first impressions are positive.

> **Good thoughts about an individual do no good unless expressed.**

31

WORK OVERTIME

WHEN

ASSUMING NEW JOB

When assuming a new job, always put in a little extra time, work and effort the first few weeks. These actions will be noticed by your superiors and your subordinates. It will make a statement as to who you are and what you expect.

In addition to the above reasons, there are many aspects of a new job with which you might not be familiar. Working extra hours in the beginning will allow you to become familiar with your total job content more quickly.

EFFECTIVE

Producing a decided, decisive,
or desired effect.

Producing the intended or expected results.

Effectual. Efficient. Efficacious.

32

SEE YOURSELF

AS OTHERS

MAY SEE YOU

___

From time to time try seeing yourself as others see you. Do you like what you see? Remember, others know you only by your actions and words. If all you are doing is going around barking orders and chewing people out when something is not perfect, you are not demonstrating very effective leadership.

People like to see caring and compassion in their leaders. Is that not what you would like to see in your boss? Self analysis can make you a better person and a better leader.

> **TEAMWORK:**
> **Partnership**
> **in**
> **harmony.**

33

DON'T FLAUNT

YOUR AUTHORITY

If you have to tell people that you are in charge, that you are their boss, you have a leadership problem. Ideally, you should not have to think about you being in charge and others should not forget that you are in charge. Work *WITH* people. Leadership comes with this responsibility.

If you are in charge, others know that fact. Do not flaunt your authority by *"barking"* orders and demanding things all the time.

"Leadership is action
not position."
DONALD McGANNON

34

MANAGE YOUR TIME

OR OTHERS WILL

MANAGE IT FOR YOU

Either you manage your time or others will manage it for you. Do not become distracted by other people or other people's concerns.

Set your schedule or agenda and stick to it. At the beginning of each day use a calendar to schedule all important events and activities. Set time limits where possible.

Do not allow others to waste your time talking about non-work subjects. You should be working when you are at work. Manage your time wisely and stay properly focused on the issues that concern you.

> **Never tell
> your boss:
> "I don't have time."**

35

HALO EFFECT

IN

PERFORMANCE APPRAISALS

This refers to letting one or two personal and/or performance traits dominate the overall evaluation of an individual. For instance, you have a person who shows up for work early and works late. A natural tendency would be to grade that person high in all graded traits. Thus, the **HALO EFFECT**. However, a person's appearance, quality of work, etc., has nothing to do with total hours worked. Each individual trait should be measured and graded separately.

36

SOMEONE WITH

NOTHING TO DO?

TAKE CORRECTIVE ACTION

If you run across someone who does not have anything to do, he or she is either lazy or does not know the full extent of his or her job. In either case, take corrective action.

If you allow anybody to walk around or sit around doing nothing, that person will soon have company. Advise people of their jobs and responsibilities and get them moving.

VISION

Something seen or perceived
in or about the future.

The act or power of imagination.

37

BE PROFESSIONAL.

CARE ABOUT

YOUR JOB

Always be a professional and care about your job. Never be indifferent about the way you do your work. You should take pride in your work and your job. Expect the same of subordinates.

Pay close attention to small details. Little jobs should be as important as the larger tasks. Make routine jobs a source of personal pride.

A professional takes great pride in completing the little jobs, the daily routine matters, and the difficult tasking with equal efficiency and effectiveness.

> "By far
> the most valuable
> possession
> is *skill*."
> HIPPARCHUS

38

OFFER NO EXCUSES

WHEN YOU

MAKE A MISTAKE

When something goes wrong, do not offer your superior excuses unless asked to do so. Respond with positive responses like:

"I'll fix it."

"I'll take care of it."

"We will correct it."

"We learned something new."

"It won't happen again."

Then fix the problem or mistake and move on to the next task.

Do not dwell on mistakes. Everybody makes them.

39

INFORM OTHERS

OF YOUR WHEREABOUTS

—

When you leave your normal work place, inform someone where you are going and when you expect to return.

If something important comes up, or if your boss is looking for you, not knowing where you are or when you might return could be disastrous.

An *AGGRESSIVE* worker
is one thing.
An *AGGRESSIVE* personality
is something else again.

40

LEADERSHIP

MEANS

"FOLLOW ME"

If leadership means anything, it means *FOLLOW ME*. That means simply to lead by example. If you want others to act or perform in a certain manner, they should be able to follow your lead.

Others will look to you for guidance and direction. Set the pace. Do not *TELL* others, *SHOW* them. Show them how to be professional. Show them what you expect.

> "No great man ever
> complains of
> want of opportunity."
> RALPH WALDO EMERSON

41

KEEP SUBORDINATES

GAINFULLY

EMPLOYED

Do not make work for work's sake. If you go through an occasional slow work period, ask your superior for additional work. You can also get with your best people to determine what to do next. This is also a good time for you to integrate some of your career goals into the workplace.

If you are good at your job you will always find something that deserves attention. Training is always time well spent. Slack periods offer an excellent opportunity to have a general meeting with your people to talk over past success and future endeavors.

Whatever avenues you take, keep your subordinates gainfully employed in meeting the goals and objectives of your organization.

Your job *is* your career.

42

MAKE DECISIONS

YOUR BOSS

WOULD MAKE

If in doubt about how to handle an unusual situation, ask yourself, "How would 'the boss' respond to this?" If you have to make a decision, you will never be too wrong if you make the decision you think your superior would make.

Follow up your decision by informing your boss of the situation and your response at the earliest opportunity. During these occasions, no one will know the situation better than you. Therefore, you should inform the boss to ensure that the correct information is passed along.

> **It is human nature to want to be recognized and rewarded for special effort or achievement.**

43

NEVER COMPLAIN

IN FRONT OF

SUBORDINATES

Never complain about something in front of subordinates. They will quickly pick up on the action. Soon, many of the people working for you will be complaining. Then you have a real morale and leadership problem.

Your actions and deeds can express your feelings to others as easily as your words. Be careful. If you develop an attitude problem about something, stay away from others until you have come to grips with the situation.

Always keep a positive attitude and outlook.

> **A successful leader is a coach and a cheerleader.**

44

EARN THE TRUST

AND CONFIDENCE

OF OTHERS

———

Earn the trust and confidence of superiors and subordinates. Show others that they can rely on you. Professionally and personally, nothing defines a person's character more than their trust and confidence.

You can accomplish many things when others have trust in you. Would you give an important job to someone you did not trust? It is doubtful. Your superiors feel the same way.

Confidence is equally as important as trust. People will almost always follow a leader in whom they have confidence. Superiors will almost always give an important job to someone who has earned their confidence.

> **All good ideas don't come from the top.**

45

OFFER YOUR OPINION,

NOT YOUR

DISAGREEMENT

In discussions with superiors, offer your opinion when the opportunity presents itself. This shows your courage, your conviction, and your interest in the subject.

If your opinion is not picked-up on, do not force the issue. To do so shows disagreement with the decision or action taken. Stated another way, it shows disagreement with the superior(s). *You can disagree without being disagreeable.*

**Want some
new answers?
Ask someone else,
not yourself.**

46

PLAN ONE

ENJOYMENT ACTIVITY

EACH DAY

Plan to do at least one thing each work day that you really enjoy. It will give you something to look forward to and keep you in good spirits during the day.

All too often people become so engrossed in their daily activities that they get into a rut. At some point the body is there but the spirit is gone. Keep your spirits high by doing something each day that you really enjoy.

CREATIVE

Marked by ability or power to create.

Given to creating.

Originality of thought, expression.

Invent. Imaginative.

47

DON'T COMPLAIN

UNLESS YOU HAVE

A CORRECTIVE SUGGESTION

Never complain about something being wrong unless you have at least one good suggestion to correct the problem or situation. Complaints do not get anything accomplished, except maybe to diminish morale.

If you think that something is bad enough that you need to complain, then you should know what you would do to correct the situation or problem. If not, do not complain.

Complaints are easy to find. Good suggestions are hard to come by. Do some research work on problem areas. Make it a point to be one person in your organization who offers corrective suggestions.

> **Good deeds must
> be supported by
> good rewards.**

48

HAVE

CONFIDENCE

IN YOURSELF

Have, and show, confidence in yourself and your abilities. You cannot be an effective leader of people without self confidence. Others can easily spot a lack of confidence.

If you are not familiar with something that requires your attention, do some research. Consider your options and come to a logical conclusion. Then, follow through on your decision with confidence.

Never place yourself in a position where you are afraid to make a decision due to lack of confidence.

> "You may pardon
> much to others,
> nothing to yourself."
> AUSONIUS

49

HANDLE

PAPERWORK

ONLY ONE TIME

———

Try to handle each piece of paperwork crossing your desk only one time; *twice at most*.

Clear your *in basket* several times a day. Some of the information crossing your desk is going to be time sensitive and important. Do not let that information become lost with the everyday paperwork.

Routinely take all of the paperwork out of your *in basket*. Have a pen or pencil in your hand and be ready to use it. Read through each piece of paper. Take some action on each document. Do not place the same piece of paper back in your *in basket*. If you personally need to do some research on a document, place that document in a *pending basket*. Do not put it back in your *in basket*. All other paperwork should be forwarded.

> **Successful people
> make their own
> opportunities.**

50

PERSONAL DATA

REFERENCE FILE

Below is a subject list of information you might want to have written down and readily available on each individual working for you.

1) Full name
2) Spouse & Children's full name
3) Home phone number
4) Home mailing address
5) Birthday dates & other special family dates
6) How long person has been with you or the organization
7) When eligible/due for promotion consideration
8) Past jobs & experiences
9) Formal education
10) Special training
11) Expected loss/transfer date
12) Hobbies, community involvement & other off-work activities
13) Past performance history
14) Individual's personal/career goals
15) Spouse's work/job, special skills and interests
16) Other information as desired

51

BE

A

ROLE MODEL

Demonstrate the behavior, attitude and skills that aid a subordinate in achieving   professional development and personal growth.

Your attitude should be that if everyone in your organization followed your lead you would have the best organization in the world.

Show people that you are a "professional." *Be a role model.* Lead the way.

DIPLOMACY

Skill in handling people so that

there is little or no ill will.

To avoid offending others.
TACT

52

TAKE WRITTEN NOTES

AT MEETINGS

Do not show up for a meeting without pen and paper. Take written notes at all meetings. Take notes of everything covered in the meeting. Go over your notes when the meeting is completed. Re-write the notes into one complete, cohesive paper that you should maintain in a file for an appropriate period of time.

Pass along all information pertinent to others as soon as possible. General information can be passed orally. More important information should be typed (memo or other appropriate vehicle) and distributed to all interested personnel.

Turn ideas into action.
Turn action into reality.

53

ASK

OTHERS

FOR INPUT

———

If something needs to be changed or updated, always ask the people doing the work for their input. They have a personal working knowledge and a personal interest in the area in question. No one else has the experience or knowledge of these first-line people.

Explain the problem or situation to your first-line people and ask them to get together and give you a consolidated input recommendation. Most of the time this input will be better than the input of someone sitting behind a desk.

> "The farther back you
> can look, the farther
> forward you are
> likely to see."
> WINSTON CHURCHILL

54

DON'T GIVE

COMPLICATED

INSTRUCTIONS

Subscribe to the **KISS** ("**K**eep **I**t **S**imple **S**tupid") Principle. Do not give complicated directions or instructions and you will not be disappointed.

Do not ask, or expect, others to remember complicated or intricate details. Tasks that take some time to complete should be reviewed with the individuals doing the work from time to time to ensure directions remain clear and in focus.

> **Share team success with the team.**

55

RESOLVE

YOUR PEOPLE'S

EMOTIONAL NEEDS

Someone with emotional needs or problems will not perform up to his/her usual standards. Be on the lookout for people with personal problems. People's emotional needs must be resolved before they can perform at full capacity.

People's outward behavior can be a clue to their emotional needs. If someone's behavior or attitude changes suddenly, that person may have an emotional need or problem.

Successful people
see opportunities,
not problems.

56

DRESS

TO

IMPRESS

Keep your personal grooming and appearance standards *above reproach.* Take your clues on how to dress by observing your superiors.

You should always dress as though you are ready to fill a higher position in your organization. Your boss should be able to look at you and say, "That person is ready to move up."

The way you dress sends a powerful message about you.

LOYAL

Faithful to a cause, idea,
custom, or allegiance.

Faithful to one's obligations,
commitments, or oath.

Fidelity.

57

DON'T GIVE

ARTIFICIALLY SHORT

DEADLINES

Give someone sufficient time to successfully complete a task or project. Placing an artificially short deadline on someone will get you a response, but it may not be the best possible response.

If you give someone 1 day to come up with a solution to a difficult situation, answer or problem, you will receive a response. You would probably receive a better response if you give the person 2 or 3 days to find solutions to difficult or complex problems.

Routinely giving people short deadlines will have a detrimental effect on morale. People who believe they are always being pushed to complete a job soon lose their enthusiasm. Declining morale will follow shortly.

58

STAY ON TOP

OF YOUR

CAREER FIELD

Read and evaluate any new information in your career field that you can find. Stay on top of new practices and procedures. Make it a point to routinely talk about subjects in your career field with others around you. Share your knowledge with them and get them to share their knowledge with you.

In today's world nothing stays the same for long. If you are not moving ahead in your career field, you are being left behind.

> Get ahead of the crowd
> if you want to
> get ahead in
> life.

59

YOU MUST BE A

GOOD FOLLOWER

TO BE A

GOOD LEADER

To be a good leader, you *must* first be a good follower. You must know what is involved in being a good follower. Sometimes it is harder to be a follower than it is to be a leader. Leaders must recognize this fact. If you cannot follow, you cannot lead.

If you find yourself questioning the authority of your superior, you are not being a good follower. If you openly question why something is being done in a particular fashion, you are not being a good follower. Once you fully understand all of the implications of being a good follower you can be a good leader.

> Success and
> hard work
> share the
> same bed.

60

PROVIDE

CHALLENGING

WORK

Provide work that stretches a subordinate's knowledge and skills in order to stimulate growth and promotion opportunities. One of your jobs as a leader is to prepare others for increased responsibility.

When you do not challenge people you do not get their best work. If you give a "hard charger" routine work you are wasting that person's time, talent and energy. People need to be challenged to do their best work.

> "Good words are worth much, and cost little."
> GEORGE HERBERT

61

YOU MUST BE ABLE

TO DO AN

"EFFECTIVE" JOB

You do not have to be the most intelligent, knowledgeable or creative person to be the *MOST* effective. Completing jobs correctly the first time is being "effective." Some people make great plans but leave the execution to others of lesser talent. They compound the error by not following up or following through on the plan. A person with less knowledge and intelligence can schedule, execute, and follow through on a plan that is less sophisticated and be more successful, or more effective.

YOUR JOB IS TO BE EFFECTIVE. If others did not think you had the ability to be effective, you would not be where you are. Do not let the intelligence of others intimidate you.

> **Give credit where
> credit is due.**

62

ASK

YOUR

PEOPLE

Ask your people questions if you want to increase the effectiveness of your organization. "Is there anything I could do for you that would make this job easier or simpler?" "Do you have any ideas on how we might improve this?" "What do you think of the way we are doing ..."

Ask questions, and listen carefully to the answers. Chances are that if you ask this type of question to different people during the week, by the end of the week you will have new, more effective ways to doing things.

Ask, listen, and then take action on any good suggestion or proposal.

> Ignorance is usually
> a self-inflicted
> wound.

63

LEARN

TO

DELEGATE

———

Learn to delegate authority to others. If you do not you may become bogged down in too many minor details. This makes it difficult to keep focused on the overall objectives of your organization.

By not allowing subordinates to assume some authority they will not grow professionally. Additionally, they will not have a personal interest in the successful completion of tasks and projects.

Remember, *YOU CAN ONLY DELEGATE THE AUTHORITY, NOT THE RESPONSIBILITY.* You remain overall responsible for all actions and tasks under your area of responsibility.

> Good leadership comes from the heart.

64

BE

HELPFUL

TO OTHERS

Helping others builds team work, morale and goodwill. Make it a point to go out of your way from time to time to help someone. You should get a good feeling about yourself when you take the time to help someone else.

If you make a sincere effort to help someone, that deed will not soon be forgotten. The help can be professional or personal. Either way, you have earned someone's loyalty and support.

HONOR

Honesty or integrity in

one's beliefs or actions.

65

PLAN

STRESS RELIEVING

ACTIVITY

Plan at least one stress-relieving activity each work day. Mid-morning or early afternoon would be the best time. Any short duration activity that will take your mind off the pressures and stress of your job will do nicely. Your blood pressure will probably drop and you will gain a new energy.

Your stress relieving activity can be anything from a short, quiet coffee break to a short non-work conversation with someone. Listening to soft music in a quiet place also relieves stress. Find something that works for you.

> People who enjoy
> their job work,
> and work and work.

66

QUALITY

NOT

QUANTITY

Do not sacrifice *QUALITY* for *QUANTITY*. Doing two or three jobs correctly is much better than doing four or five jobs half-way. If you do not have time to do a job correctly the first time, when are you going to find time to do it again?

Save time, energy and effort by doing a job correctly the first time. At the same time you will not have your boss questioning your work habits.

If your people see you not giving your best effort, they will soon follow your lead. Do quality work the first time, all the time.

> **The louder you talk,
> the angrier
> you become.**

67

MAKE EYE CONTACT

WHEN TALKING

TO OTHERS

When talking to someone, always make, and keep, eye contact with that person. This action shows your concern and attention to the matter at hand.

Failure to maintain eye contact is perceived as being weak, timid or unsure of yourself. No one can be an effective leader with any of these shortcomings.

"There is nothing so powerful as truth--and often nothing so strange."
DANIEL WEBSTER

68

WHEN SOMEONE

OFFERS ADVICE,

LISTEN

When someone offers you advice, listen intently and do not become defensive. Evaluate what you heard and determine if there was any validity to the advice offered. Becoming defensive will stop any hope of future advice. We can all learn from others if we simply pay attention.

Always consider the source of the advice. Do not take advice from superiors lightly. Listen to people with more knowledge and experience than yourself. Listen, but be skeptical, to advice from those with less knowledge or experience than yourself.

> **Quality control *work* should start before quality control *checks*.**

69

KEEP SPIRITS

OF YOUR PEOPLE

HIGH

People rarely succeed at anything unless they can enjoy themselves in the process. No one enjoys doing something they do not like. It is a leader's responsibility to put fun, enjoyment and excitement in the daily work schedule.

Find a way to break others out of mundane day-to-day work. Inject a little humor from time to time. Do something to get the people to pull together for a common cause or challenge.

Make work enjoyable. Keep spirits high.

> **Good treatment
> leads to
> good morale.**

70

SHOW

UP

EARLY

Be a few minutes early for work, meetings, etc. Being early shows your care and interest. During this extra time you can usually pick up a little extra information in the process.

If you show up early for a meeting you can usually talk personally with the person conducting the meeting. Sometimes you can get more information, or insight, in this conversation than at the meeting itself.

> Know WHAT to say.
> Know WHEN to say it.
> More importantly,
> Know WHEN to say nothing.

71

TEAMWORK

Teamwork is people working together for a common cause, objective or purpose. To improve teamwork a leader should promote *harmony, cooperation* and *understanding.*

Tell, and show, people that they are an important member of *the team.* Acknowledge individual contributions to the team.

Reinforce commitment to excellence and loyalty. Stress professionalism and performance.

Use the words *"team"* and *"teamwork"* frequently in conversations with team members. Say *"we"* and *"us,"* not *"me"* or *"they."*

Plan an occasional off-work activity get-together for team members only. Ask the team members what they would like to do. Have the members of the team plan and organize the event or activity. This secures their wholehearted support and cooperation.

72

HONOR

YOUR

PEOPLE

If you do not honor people, they will not honor you. Honor is a two-way street. Displaying honor and respect is one of the quickest ways to gain the willing support of others.

If you respect people for what they are and what they do, you honor them. Acknowledge the accomplishments of others and you honor them.

EFFICIENT

Productive of desired results.

Productive without waste.

Performing in best possible
and least wasteful manner.

Economical use. Effective.

73

SEEK

OUT

OPPORTUNITIES

———

Be on the lookout for opportunities. Even small opportunities can lead to great achievements. Completing your daily, routine tasks in timely and correct fashion is your most important job. The people who are successful in this area receive the more important *"big"* jobs when they present themselves. That is opportunity.

There are always opportunities waiting to be found. Find something that should be done and you have found an opportunity. Doing something that others failed to do is opportunity.

When opportunity knocks, be there and be ready.

> **If you have only short-range goals, you are not looking far enough ahead.**

74

PRIORITIZE

YOUR

TASKS

Always put your jobs and tasks in priority order. Everything should be written down on paper. This includes the long-range tasking and the daily jobs. Every job should have a priority assigned. Do not allow yourself or your people to waste time on low priority tasking when a higher priority exists.

Every morning make sure that you and your people start work on the highest priority jobs first.

> "Obstacles are those frightening things you see when you take your eyes off the goal."
> HANNAH MOORE

75

GET YOUR PEOPLE

INVOLVED &

MOTIVATED

Get everyone in your organization personally involved in important goals and objectives. Explain why a job is important and necessary. Give them the necessary information and then ask them for their suggestions. Give people a reason to become personally involved and motivated.

Remember, people are more motivated about the *OUTCOME* of a job or project when they have an *INPUT*.

The fire of mediocrity is
fueled by maintaining
the status quo.

76

SHOW OTHERS

YOU CARE

ABOUT THEM

When you have newly reported personnel working for you, make it a point to check with them periodically. Ask how things are going, if they are having any problems or difficulties, etc.

In your daily activities take the time to ask others how things are going. Ask them if they require any assistance. Ask, and care about, their off-work activities and interests.

Do not just tell people you care; show people that you care about them personally.

```
If you brag
about yourself,
others won't.
```

77

MAKE SOMEONE

"WANT"

TO DO SOMETHING

Remember, you can generally **MAKE** a subordinate do something. In this case, when you are out of sight and out of mind, the effort may cease. Leadership is **MAKING SOMEONE "WANT TO DO" SOMETHING**. The effort continues when you are not around in this case.

Supply others with whatever motivation it takes to make them want to do something.

PRAISE

To express a favorable judgment.

An expression of approval.

Commend. Commendation.

78

TELL PEOPLE

"WHAT" AND "WHY"

THEY NEED TO KNOW

———

When you are talking to someone about a subject or project, do not tell that person everything you know. That takes too much time and generally confuses the issue. Tell them *WHAT* they need to know, and *WHY* it is important to them. This action saves time and energy.

"There are no bad soldiers, only bad officers."
NAPOLEON

79

KEEP A LIST

OF EMERGENCY

PHONE NUMBERS

———

Maintain an up-to-date, comprehensive list of emergency phone numbers that may be required on short notice (fire, ambulance, etc.). The list should include all emergency services and any individuals who may need to be notified of an emergency.

You should never be very far away from this emergency phone list. Keep a copy at work, at home, and either in your car or on your person at all times. When you need this list, you need it now, now an hour from now.

> **Loyalty is a two-way street.**

80

LEADERSHIP PRINCIPLES

THE "WINNER" VS. THE "LOSER"

A *WINNER* says, "Let's find out."
A *LOSER* says, "Nobody knows."

When a *WINNER* makes a mistake, he/she says, "I was wrong."
When a *LOSER* makes a mistake, he/she says, "It wasn't my fault."

A *WINNER* isn't nearly as afraid of losing as
A *LOSER* is secretly afraid of winning.

A *WINNER* works harder than a loser and has more time.
A *LOSER* is always "too busy" to do what is necessary.

A *WINNER* goes through a problem;
A *LOSER* goes around it, and never gets past it.

A *WINNER* paces himself or herself;
A *LOSER* has only two speeds--hysterical and lethargic.

A *WINNER* make commitments;
A *LOSER* makes promises.

A *WINNER* says, "I am good, but not as good as I ought to be."
A *LOSER* says, "I'm not as bad as a lot of other people."

A *WINNER* listens;
A *LOSER* just waits until it's his/her turn to talk.

A *WINNER* respects those who are superior and tries to learn something from them;
A *LOSER* resents those who are superior, and tries to find chinks in their armor.

A *WINNER* explains;
A *LOSER* explains away.

A *WINNER* sees responsible for more than the job;
A *LOSER* says, "I only work here."

A *WINNER* says, "There ought to be a better way to do it."
A *LOSER* says, "That's the way it's always been done."

81

KEEP MEETINGS

ON TRACK &

ON SCHEDULE

If you schedule a meeting, set a specific *START* and *STOP* time. Keep the discussions on track with why the meeting was scheduled in the first place. Otherwise, meetings have a tendency to run on without end.

If you want to assure that a meeting is kept short, schedule it just before the end of the work day. If the work day ends at 4:30 p.m., schedule the meeting for 4:00 p.m. There is very little chance that this meeting will last longer than 30 minutes.

"The best test
of a man is
authority."
PROVERB

82

PROOF-READ

DOCUMENTS

BEFORE YOU SIGN

———

Carefully proof-read all written documents and correspondence before you place your signature on them. When you affix your signature to something, be sure you know exactly what you are signing.

Read important documents carefully. Analyze each page paragraph by paragraph. Again, read the document on more than one occasion.

> **STRESS:**
> **What people**
> **place on themselves**
> **to make something seem**
> **more difficult.**

83

SHARE

"WELL DONE"

WITH YOUR TEAM

———

Anytime you get a "*well done*," share it with the people working for you. Inform your people that "we" as a team earned the "well done."

When you receive a "well done" from your superior, gather your people around you and tell them about it. Tell them their effort and work is appreciated. Turn a "well done" into a teamwork morale booster.

RESPONSIBILITY

Moral, legal, or mental accountability.

Burden of obligation.

Being responsible.

84

WHO

REALLY DESTROYS

ORGANIZATION EFFECTIVENESS?

Incompetent people do not destroy an organization. They never attain a high enough position. The people who have achieved something in the past and earned promotion, and then rest on the past, do the most damage to an organization.

Keep your eyes and ears open. Do not allow people who have been successful in the past to rest on their laurels. Give them challenges. Be sure they are thinking about the future.

> **Emulate those who stand above the rest in *courage, honesty* and *loyalty*.**

85

ALWAYS

REWARD

GOOD PERFORMANCE

If you reward someone for their good performance, that performance will likely be repeated. *Also*, this performance may be repeated by more than one person the next time.

Fail to reward someone for good performance and that performance may or may not be repeated. People want to be recognized when they do a good job.

Always recognize and reward good performance.

> People learn from their mistakes.
> If you haven't made one recently, you
> haven't learned much.

86

APPLY & ENFORCE

LEADERSHIP

CONSISTENTLY

———

Be consistent. *Leadership must be applied and enforced consistently.* Do not send mixed signals to those working for you. Being cheerful and lax one day and strict the next day will leave people unsure about themselves, their work, and you.

People who do something right should know what to expect from you. Just as importantly, people who do something wrong should know what to expect from you. That is consistent leadership.

> **Potential itself never accomplished anything.**

87

SET & MAINTAIN

REALISTIC

GOALS

Set and attain realistic goals for yourself and others. If goals are unachievable or unrealistic, enthusiasm will quickly dissipate and morale will suffer.

This does not mean to set easily achievable goals. Goals should be demanding, just not too demanding.

You should remember a goal is a minimum standard. If someone gives you two weeks to accomplish a task and you take two weeks to complete the task, you met the goal. If you would have completed the task in less than two weeks you would have exceeded the goal. Try to exceed goals given to you by other people.

> **To expand your horizon, open your ears and eyes.**

88

TAKE

PAPERWORK

HOME

There are times when you may have a particularly busy schedule. When these occasions arise, try to do some of your paperwork outside normal work hours. This will help you to keep on schedule.

Working on paperwork in a quiet place where you are not subject to interruption becomes easier and quicker.

Many successful leaders routinely take paperwork home. This action prevents them from being tied to their desk all day and allows them to do what they are supposed to do-- *LEAD*.

> "All problems become smaller if you
> don't dodge them but
> confront them."
> ADMIRAL WILLIAM F. HALSEY

89

ADMIT

·MISTAKES

EARLY

———

Admit any mistakes or errors early, before they get out of hand. Take minor corrective steps immediately before they become major problems.

Remember, *no one* has *all* the right answers. Some mistakes are expected. Simply correct them and move on to the next task.

Mistakes should surface as soon as possible to minimize damage. Show others that you are not afraid to admit mistakes and they will be more inclined to tell you when they make a mistake.

> **Cheerful people spread cheerfulness. Unhappy people spread unhappiness.**

90

LET OTHERS KNOW

THEY CAN DEPEND ON YOU

Show others they can depend on you, any time, all the time. If you need an important job completed, you should always give it to someone dependable. Your superiors feel the same way. *Be dependable.*

Being dependable is more important than having skill or talent. Skill and talent are only *"potential."* To be *"dependable"* means to get the job successfully completed.

Most people can
learn more if
they are exposed
to more.

91

GO

EXTRA MILE

WHEN NECESSARY

Push yourself to the limit when it is really important. Demonstrate to others that when the chips are down, you are there.

If you need to speed up your work schedule, do it. If you need to work late occasionally, do it. People who do not give a little extra effort when it is required will never climb high on the promotion ladder.

Show others that you are ready, willing and able to give an extra effort whenever it is required.

> **Self-discipline
> is the best
> discipline
> of all.**

92

HAVE A

POSITIVE DESK

IMAGE

Your desk reflects on you personally. A neat and tidy desk reflects a neat and tidy person. A cluttered desk reflects something else.

Do not allow pending paperwork to collect in stacks on your desk. If you have paperwork on on-going or pending projects, place it in the file or in your desk.

Always present a positive image of yourself whenever possible.

DELEGATING

Providing the *RESOURCES* and

AUTHORITY to someone who

has the *ABILITY*.

93

HAVE A

POSITIVE OFFICE

IMAGE

If you have pictures on your desk or your office, make sure they present a positive image of you. A picture of your family on your desk is a good, positive image. If you are not married, a picture of your pet or your car will do nicely. A picture postcard will also fill the bill.

For the office a job oriented picture or two projects a good image. As a final touch, have an appropriate saying or quote posted somewhere in your office. This should be something that reflects your personality. Think of the immediate perception someone might have of you when you have one of the following statements posted in your office.

"LEAD, FOLLOW, OR GET OUT OF THE WAY"
"ACTION, NOT WORDS"
"DO IT RIGHT THE FIRST TIME"
"THE BUCK STOPS HERE"
Etc.

Your office, like your desk, should be maintained in a clean and orderly fashion.

94

EXPAND YOUR

PROFESSIONAL DEVELOPMENT

EACH DAY

Make it a point to do something to increase your professional development each day. It should be in a specific area where you want to improve yourself: People, equipment, learn a new word, etc. Place a cryptic message on your calendar as a reminder if necessary.

In today's world any information you learned over five years ago is most likely obsolete. That means that if you are not continually improving your professional development you will someday become obsolete.

> **LEADERSHIP:**
> **Setting the**
> **vision and**
> **the course.**

95

TOO MUCH SOCIALIZING

WITH JUNIORS IS HARMFUL

Be careful about socializing too much with juniors in or outside the work place. Becoming too friendly makes leadership more difficult. There will always be some people who will try to take advantage of a friendship. It is good to be friendly. It is not so good to be too friendly.

Becoming too friendly with a few people can be perceived as showing favoritism. Showing favoritism will surely lead to resentment and a drop in morale.

Friendship should not come into play when making leadership or management decisions.

"When you betray someone else, you also betray yourself."
ISAAC BASHEVIS SINGER

96

ACKNOWLEDGE

ASSISTANCE

OF PEERS

Ensure that help or assistance from a peer or co-worker is publicly acknowledged in the presence of the peer and his or her superior. This shows your gratitude and appreciation, and helps ensure continued cooperation and assistance in the future. It also builds on morale and reinforces the concept of teamwork.

Make decisions when it is
time to make decisions.
Not too early.
Not too late.
Make timely decisions on time.

97

DON'T

MISS

DEADLINES

Do not miss the deadline of a superior. If a problem arises, advise that superior before the deadline and work together on a solution. There should be no reason to surprise your superior with an incomplete job.

To miss a deadline shows that you are not dependable.

SELF-CONFIDENCE

Realistic and objective

confidence in one's own

judgment and ability.

98

MAINTAIN CLOSE

WORKING

RELATIONSHIPS

———

A close working relationship with others can be your best source of information about what is going on around you. *Good decisions require good information.*

Pass information along to your peers and request the same of them. Ask others to keep you informed of any up-coming important events or activities.

Cultivate close working relationships at every opportunity.

> **Break large jobs down into small, individual pieces.**

99

DOCUMENT

SUPERIOR & SUBSTANDARD

PERFORMANCE

Document the superior or substandard performance demonstrated by those who work for you immediately. Do not wait.

Superior performance should be recognized and rewarded immediately. Substandard performance should be corrected as soon as possible. Let everyone know when they are doing superior or substandard work.

> **Self-imposed limitations keep most people from moving forward.**

100

MAINTAIN

YOUR OWN

"BRAG" FILE

You should maintain a personal "*brag file*." Place anything in this file that reflects favorably upon you. Include accomplishments, achievements, actions, events, correspondence, education, and so forth. Use dates and names as necessary.

You should have a short-term and a long term brag file. Short-term file information can be used at performance appraisal times and similar events.

Place material of possible historical information or value to you personally in a permanent long-term brag file.

> You cannot learn much
> when you are talking.
> You can learn a lot
> by just listening.

101

BECOME INVOLVED

IN

COMMUNITY ACTIVITIES

First, everyone should want to actively participate in community activities and events. Becoming involved in these endeavors helps make you a better rounded person. This also gives you an opportunity to meet with other professional people.

Second, if for no other reason, it looks good on your record to be a person with diverse interests and talents.

Get yourself and others involved in some community activities of choice.

> **"So much of what we call management consists of making it difficult for people to work."**
> **PETER DRUCKER**

102

MENTALLY PREPARE

FOR

UNEXPECTED SITUATIONS

Use otherwise idle time to mentally go over unexpected situations that could occur within your area of responsibility. Cover realistic and unrealistic situations. Sooner or later you are going to be faced with making a decision not a part of everyday responsibilities.

Many people have earned a promotion because they took the right course of action when faced with an unusual situation.

Be prepared to act when an unusual situation occurs.

> **Watch for polite hints from your boss on your performance.**

103

BE

SELF-MOTIVATED

Others can try to motivate you, but the real bottom line is that no one is really motivated until they are *SELF-MOTIVATED*. No external force can make you *WANT* to be motivated. You have to become self-motivated to succeed, to achieve anything in life.

Nothing worth having comes without applying self-motivation. Find ways to get, and stay, self-motivated.

Very few people reach their full potential without finding ways to become, and stay, self-motivated.

Do not try to fill someone
else's shoes.
Do your own thing,
create your own niche.

104

BRAINSTORM

NEW & BETTER

IDEAS

During idle times, allow yourself to brainstorm better ways of doing things. Make notes. If any of the ideas you come up with look good a couple of days later, give them more detailed thought and consideration. Involve others in the process. Write down possible actions and study them.

The more diverse your area of responsibility, the more you should be able to brainstorm and come up with new ideas, or new and more efficient ways of doing things.

Never be satisfied with the status quo. Always be on the lookout for ways and means to make improvements throughout your area of responsibility.

> **Less challenging work means less rewards.**

105

ASK & TELL

LEADERSHIP STYLE

1st - ASK someone to do something. If that does not work;

2nd - TELL someone to do something. If that does not work;

3rd - TAKE appropriate action.

People do not want to be ordered to do something. They would rather be asked. Start by asking people.

Develop a
magnetic personality.
Draw people to you.

106

SUCCESS

TAKES

DEDICATION

———

If it were easy to be successful, everybody would be successful. It takes dedication, effort and perseverance. People who do an average day's work become average performers. Average people do not become successful. They become average. If you want to get ahead, you have to perform above the average. You have to become dedicated to your job.

You need to work intelligently, harder, and put in longer hours than the average person to become highly successful. In other words, you have to dedicate yourself to your job.

Don't *TACKLE* your work, *CONQUER* it.

107

SMILE,

EVERYONE

WILL FEEL BETTER

Make it a point to smile whenever you enter an office or work space. This puts others at ease and it shows that you are approachable. You should also smile often during the day. It takes very little time and effort. You and your subordinates will feel better.

Smiling puts a positive outlook on daily activities.

Smile and the world smiles with you. Frown and you frown alone.

Having a voice in the decision stimulates the action.

108

ESTABLISH

BENCHMARK

STANDARDS & CRITERIA

Every organization needs some way to judge its performance. Individual performance must be measured against some standard, or norm, to have any real meaning. Most organizations measure individual and team performance using statistics. However, many organizations go years without giving any thought to up-dating their performance standards and job criteria.

Periodically review all written standards for your organization and all job performance criteria for your people. Chances are these have not changed in years while the organization's mission, goals and objectives have undergone significant change.

Take the initiative. Collect data, statistics, and any other information available. *ESTABLISH NEW BENCHMARK STANDARDS.* You cannot meet today's challenges and requirements using yesterday's standards.

109

NO ORGANIZATION ASSETS

FOR

PERSONAL MATTERS

Do not use organization equipment or assets for private matters. To do so is not appropriate and it is unprofessional. It also sets a bad example for others.

"Anyone who stops learning
is old,
whether at twenty or eighty.
Anyone who keeps learning
stays young."
HENRY FORD.

110

FIRST IDENTIFY,

THEN FIX

PROBLEMS

———

Carefully define a problem area before jumping in to fix it. Check with the personnel involved about a possible solution. A hasty "fix" can be worse than no fix at all.

When attempting to fix a problem area, follow the correct steps.

1st STEP - COLLECT INFORMATION
    a) *Observation*
    b) *Questions*

2nd STEP - IDENTIFY PROBLEM/CAUSE

3rd STEP - DETERMINE SOLUTION

4th STEP - IMPLEMENT ACTION

5th STEP - FOLLOW-UP & FEEDBACK

111

MAINTAIN AN ADMINISTRATIVE

REFERENCE LIBRARY

You need a reference library if you or your people perform administrative functions. Keep an up-to-date set of reference books readily available if you or your people are involved in written correspondence. Include such items as a dictionary, thesaurus, correspondence manual and samples of previously approved or used correspondence in your related area or field.

Always be prepared to work on the administrative side of your job.

People appreciate being appreciated.

112

BUILD A

PERSONAL

PROFESSIONAL LIBRARY

Build up a professional library of your own. Purchase job related books. Cut out or reproduce articles from professional publications that are of interest to you (papers, magazines, etc.). You are building on your future. Be sure to include articles that may be of some use to you in the future. Too much information is better than not enough.

Your personal professional library must be maintained up-to-date to be of any benefit to you.

Maintain a personal professional library until you retire.

> **"Be just and fear not."**
> **WILLIAM SHAKESPEARE**

113

KEEP YOUR EYE

ON THE

"BIG PICTURE"

The *"big picture"* refers to the overall mission and goals of the organization. A good organizer keeps an eye on the *"big picture"* while juggling individual components until they all fit. A bad organizer jumps on the first job that comes along just to become started and stay busy.

A manager's first job is to keep in touch with the overall objectives of the organization, and to manage things, events and activities within that framework.

Stay in close communications with others in your organization to ensure that when changes in the "big picture" occur you can adjust your schedule and priorities accordingly.

> **"We must all do what
> we can
> with what we have."
> WW II Navy quote.**

114

MAINTAIN

A LONG-RANGE

CHECK-LIST

Keep a written, up-to-date check-list of long-range goals and objectives of your organization. The list should include items handed down from above and your own agenda for your organization. Check on the progress of these projects regularly. This list should be prioritized in work order.

The jobs and tasks handed down to you usually do not encompass areas that need correction or updating within your own particular organization to function efficiently. Add items you consider necessary to your organization to the list of items handed down to you.

> Enhance relationships
> and you enhance
> teamwork.

115

MAINTAIN A

SHORT-RANGE

CHECK-LIST

In addition to maintaining a list of long-range goals and objectives, keep a short-range list of jobs to accomplish. This should be a weekly list, updated daily. Add new items as they surface. Delete completed items.

Jobs written down on paper have a better chance of being remembered and completed.

There are going to be times when you finish your week's work early. When you do the short-range check-list is a good place to add items to improve the efficiency of your organization. That would be the items you initially placed on your long-range check-list.

> **Honesty is the personal trait most favored by others.**

116

ENTHUSIASM

AS IMPORTANT

AS ABILITY

Be proud of what you do and be energetic about your work. *Enthusiasm is contagious.* Having enthusiasm about a job is almost as important as having the ability to do the work.

It is easy to spot people who are, and people who are not, enthusiastic about their work. People cannot do a top quality job unless they are enthusiastic about their work. Find a way, or reason, to become enthusiastic. Pass this enthusiasm along to the people working for you.

RESPECT

Esteem for worth or excellence
of personal quality or trait.

To consider worthy of high
or special regard.

Esteem.

117

USE

MORNING ENERGY

FOR TOUGH JOBS

Tackle the toughest job of the day the first thing in the morning. This is when most people feel more energetic. You are going to be at least partially preoccupied with the task if you put it off until later in the day.

Your energy, and that of the people working for you, will slowly drain during the day. Afternoon results may not be as good as morning results.

Consistent leadership removes much confusion, doubt and misunderstanding.

118

SURROUND YOURSELF

WITH YOUR

BEST PEOPLE

Surround yourself with the best people available. Place these people in your "*inner circle*" of organizational influence. This should be your most professional and knowledgeable people. You want your top professional people around you to help supply you with correct information and to help you make decisions.

Ask more of your best people. Ask them to give you all they have. When you get it, reward them. Give them room to operate and grow professionally. These people are your "*hard chargers*," let them charge ahead.

> **Want to
> get ahead?
> Plan ahead.**

119

ASSIGN TASKS

TO SOMEONE

WHO IS INTERESTED

Assign specific tasks to individuals who have some interest (personal or professional) in the task. If someone does not have an interest in a job, see that you arouse his or her interest in the subject before the task is started.

Be careful not to give all the tough jobs to the same few energetic people. Energetic people always seem to have more interest in working than non-energetic people. Find a way to motivate the non-energetic people. Do not let them get by with all of the easy, simple tasks.

> "What makes greatness is
> starting something that
> lives after you."
> RALPH W. SOCKMAN

120

LET OTHERS KNOW

WHAT YOU

EXPECT

———

When you first take charge of any organization, regardless of the size, let the people know up front what kind of organization you expect and what is expected from them. Give them a challenge. Present this information in a straight forward manner. You must be clear about your expectations.

Let everyone know that you expect the highest professional performance and the highest professional standards. If you do not expect excellence, you will not receive it. Tell your people that you have confidence in them and in their abilities. Get people started on a positive note.

> **If you are not moving ahead,
> you are falling behind.**

121

PROVIDE

POSITIVE

REINFORCEMENT

Timing is the key in rewarding someone for stellar performance. One of the first things you want to do when taking over a new organization is to reward someone for an individual accomplishment. When one of your *hard chargers* meets your expectations in a particular area, be quick to reward that individual.

The accomplishment may merit a verbal praise in front of others, a letter, or a higher reward. However, give only the appropriate recognition. By rewarding an individual for his or her performance you reinforce your commitment to your original expectations. Others will soon follow the lead of your first hard charger.

Motivation equals success.

122

DATE

& SIGN

ALL MEMOS

___

All notes and memos you send out should be dated and signed. This action can help avoid confusion.

Dated material also serves as a historical   reference or record.

| MOTIVATION |

The act or process of motivating.

A motivating force,

stimulus, or influence.

123

BE READY TO GO

FIRST THING

IN THE MORNING

Plan some kind of early morning, before-work physical exercise. People who do physical exercises in the morning report for work wide awake mentally and ready to go to work physically. They are energetic and ready to tackle any assignment. That should be you.

Leaders, like farmers,
reap what they sew.

124

DO NOT

SHOW

FAVORITISM

———

Do not show favoritism. The one(s) you favor will take advantage of the situation and the ones not receiving it will take offense. Dissent will quickly spread through your organization.

Be equally careful that there is no perception of favoritism. If you spend too much of your time around just a few of your people, it will be perceived as favoritism.

Rewards and discipline most of all must be handed out without favoritism.

> **"Every man loves what he is good at."**
> **THOMAS SHADWELL**

125

LEARN

FROM

MISTAKES

Failure teaches you how to be successful. *Don't be afraid to make a mistake.* People who do not do things because they are afraid they will make a mistake never accomplish anything useful.

If you want to challenge yourself to grow you must be willing to take a chance. When you take chances you make mistakes. Start by taking small chances. That means small mistakes. Learn as you go. However, be quick to identify a mistake and take corrective action immediately.

People do not learn anything when they do something correctly.

Most people learn from their own mistakes. *A smart person can learn from the mistakes of others.*

126

KNOW

FUNDAMENTAL

PERSONAL DESIRES

The three fundamental desires of a person are:

1st - *BE UNDERSTOOD*

2nd - *BE ACCEPTED*

3rd - *BE RECOGNIZED FOR ACCOMPLISHMENTS*

Knowing people's desires and how to put these desires to good use should help you as a leader.

> **Do not agitate your enemies with words.**

127

MOST PEOPLE

ARE OPPOSED

TO CHANGE

Almost everyone dislikes change. Most people feel initial discomfort and disorientation when changes are made. When you make a change in people's work content or environment, take time to ensure they understand what is happening and why.

Solicit and secure the support of your key personnel to help implement changes. Explain what you are doing and ask for their support and assistance. Most of all, ask these key people to provide you with feedback You want feedback on what effect the changes are having and how the changes are perceived by others in your organization.

> **Don't tell *me* I did a good job. Tell my boss.**

128

DON'T

SURROUND YOURSELF

WITH FLATTERERS

One of the worst advisors a leader can have is a flatterer. Almost everyone likes to be flattered. The flatterers look for an easy target--their boss. Flatterers are mostly concerned with themselves. They want to get to the top without making any waves, without questioning decisions of superiors. You do not want flatterers around you.

To achieve maximum success and professional growth, a leader needs someone around who will occasionally question a decision and offer constructive comments.

> Spread good news around.
> Keep bad news
> under wraps.

129

SHOW

INTEREST

IN OTHERS

Take the time to show your people that you care about them, that you have an interest in them personally. Showing an interest in people helps elicit their willing support.

There are many ways to show interest in others. For example, ask subordinates how something works. This action helps demonstrate your interest in them and in their work. It also makes the people you ask feel better about themselves because they have a chance to show the "boss" how much they know. You will learn something about the people and the subject in the bargain.

> **You are either a part
> of the solution, or you
> are a part of the problem.**

130

WORK ON

PRIVATE MATTERS

IN PRIVATE

Private and personal paperwork should always be worked on in private. Find a quiet place where you will not be disturbed. This includes personal matters and such official items as performance appraisals, personnel placement, etc.

DO NOT LEAVE PRIVATE OR PERSONAL PAPERWORK UNATTENDED, either on your desk or in your "in basket." Store this material under lock and key. Simply putting it in your desk or some other out-of-the way place is not sufficient. If just one person views your personal or private paperwork chances are that many will hear about the contents.

> Ask a different person
> for a new idea or
> suggestion--every day.

131

ONE

QUIET HOUR

PER DAY

Set aside one hour a day in your office when no one, except your boss, can disturb you. Close your office door. Do not accept any telephone calls or personal visits.

The one hour of quiet time effectively isolates you from the normal daily noise and activities around you. This hour can be used for almost anything that requires uninterrupted concentration. The hour can be used to go over plans, projects, priorities, personnel placement, etc.

With just one quiet hour per day in your office, you should be able to complete an amazing amount of work.

> "A man who is always ready to believe what is told him will never do well."
> GAIUS PETRONIUS

132

FORWARD

PERSONAL AWARDS

WHEN DESERVED

Know how to submit award recommendations. Deserving people should not miss out on an award or a reward just because you do not have the necessary reference material. Reluctance to draft and submit the necessary paperwork is no excuse for not doing your job as a leader.

Maintain an up-to-date file of all reference material required to draft award recommendations. Include examples of past write-ups when possible.

> Leadership
> also means to stay
> out of the way.

133

LEADERSHIP

IS A FUNCTION OF

INTERPERSONAL RELATIONSHIPS

———

Interpersonal relationships are a fundamental requirement of good leadership. Leadership is working with, and communicating with, people. Your leadership and management tasks cannot be completed without the help of others. The better you work with, and communicate with others, the more efficient you can become in carrying out your assigned duties.

Even the leader is a member of the team. Work with others. Encourage your people to work with each other, to understand each other. Stress team effort and harmony.

RESOURCEFUL

Able to deal skillfully and
promptly with new situations.

Capable of devising ways and means.

134

FRIENDLY

COMPETITION

IS GOOD

Competition in an organization is healthy as long as it stays friendly. However, too much competition between groups that must function together results in loss of cooperation and team work. Occasional competition is a good thing. Too much day-in, day-out competition will wear most people down in the long run.

Remember, within most organizations cooperation and teamwork are better than competition in the long term. With internal competition, someone always loses and resents that fact. Keep internal competition friendly when possible.

> **Focus on results,
> not *activity*.**

135

SELF-DISCIPLINE

IS THE KEY

TO SUCCESS

———

Self-discipline is doing what *NEEDS* to be done, not what you *WANT* to do. Set yourself a course and stick to it. If you know where you want to go, you should know what it takes to get there.

Self-discipline sometimes requires self-sacrifice. To sacrifice something to achieve something worth while *is* self-discipline. Develop self-discipline to learn how to stay focused on what is really important.

> **Leadership is**
> **something**
> **you do *with* people,**
> **not *to* people.**

136

KNOW WHAT'S EXPECTED

OF YOU

ALL THE TIME

―――――

If you are assigned a task, be sure to find out exactly what is expected of you (time factor, outcome, etc.). When you assign someone a task, provide the same pertinent information.

Ensure you have a written, up-to-date job description. If new tasking is assigned to you or your people, your job description may need to be updated. If in doubt, ask.

RESOLUTE

Firmly resolved or determined.

Marked by firm determination.

Bold. Steady.

137

DO NOT

GIVE

HASTY PROMISES

In your haste to impress your boss, do not promise anything that you cannot deliver. Carefully consider all tasking aspects before making a commitment. A quick "yes" could make you look good for five minutes, followed by looking bad for a very long time.

You should volunteer for extra work and projects when possible. Just be sure you know what tasking is involved *before* you volunteer.

To *really* get ahead always do more, more of everything.

138

SUBMIT

YOUR GOOD IDEAS

IN WRITING

If you have what you think is a good idea for a change or improvement, submit it to your superior in writing. This will give you a chance to make sure you say exactly what you want to say.

A written report will not be as immediately dismissed or forgotten by a superior as a verbal report. Some kind of response will be needed. This will ensure that the superior gives your idea due consideration on one or more occasions. *However*, do not flood your superior with a never-ending flow of paperwork on ideas and suggestions.

> "Energy and persistence
> conquer all things."
> BENJAMIN FRANKLIN

139

BECOME SUBORDINATE

MENTOR

When you are in charge of an organization, challenge yourself to personally take charge of the development and promotion of your few truly top performers. Become their mentor. Give them challenging work assignments to stimulate professional growth.

Reward others accordingly for their accomplishments. Make it your personal goal to see that they are on the top of the promotion list.

Losers lose opportunities.
Winners create opportunities.

140

"HOW" AND "WHAT" OF

VERBAL COMMUNICATIONS

In verbal communications, *HOW* you say something is just as important as *WHAT* you say. The tone and volume of your voice, your visual expressions and personal movements are all a part of verbal communications.

Your voice and personal gestures will tell people if you are not enthusiastic or sincere about something. When you need to communicate something to others, be sure you are in the correct mood.

"Do your duty and leave the rest to heaven."
PIERRE CORNEILLE

141

SUPERIORS

DON'T LIKE

SURPRISES

Keep superiors informed of important situations and developments as they are unfolding. Do not surprise them all at once with bad or unexpected news.

If there is a surprise about something in your organization, you should be the one to personally tell the boss. Do not let the information filter up and do not task a subordinate to deliver the news.

It is better for your boss to be over informed as opposed to being under informed.

> **"It's always been done this way" is a good indication that a change is in order.**

142

ALLOW YOURSELF TIME

TO MAKE

MAJOR DECISIONS

Do not make major decisions in a hurry. If time permits, think about the *pros* and *cons* of different possible decision results for a day or two. Decisions on major projects or goals should not be made overnight. Decisions concerning personnel should not be made in haste.

Anyone can make a decision. It's having to live with the results that are sometimes difficult. Take your time and select the best course of action.

Never make a decision when you are tired, upset, or angry.

Some people brighten up a room
when they enter,
others when they leave.

143

PERSONAL

MATTERS

—

Keep personal phone calls to an absolute minimum during work hours. If you are at work, you should be working.

Do not spend too much time talking with friends about events and activities not connected with work.

Do not set a bad example for others.

When you make people feel better about themselves, you are building on morale.

144

PROVIDE

VISION TO OTHERS

FOR INCREASED MOTIVATION

A leader should be able to have a vision about the future. Picture something better in the future. Give your vision of the future to your people in such a way that it will motivate them to put forth their best effort.

You need to see into the future before you can plan on how to get there. Most people who know where they are going find a way to get there. Show others the way, and then lead them.

> Routine
> work
> breeds
> routine
> performance.

145

WRITE DOWN

MESSAGES

TO OTHER PEOPLE

If you are asked to pass a message along to someone else, write it down on paper. Make sure all pertinent information is covered.

If the message was received via telephone, write down the correct spelling of the person who called. Ask the person if you need to write down his or her telephone number.

You should consider all messages important. Ensure all information is passed along in a timely fashion.

SELF-DISCIPLINE

Discipline and training of oneself.

Regulation of oneself for
the sake of improvement.

146

ASK FOR FEEDBACK

FOR BETTER

DECISION-MAKING

An organization cannot function smoothly and effectively without a steady stream of two-way communications. Much of the information being passed upward should be feedback on how things are, or are not, functioning effectively.

Ask for feedback. If people do not willingly provide you with information, ask for it. Get information from all levels of your organization. You cannot make good decisions based on bad or incomplete information.

TEAM PLAYER: Ask yourself what you can contribute that is not a part of your job description.

147

ALLOW

SUBORDINATES

A POLICY VOICE

To build on teamwork and secure loyalty, allow key subordinates a voice in policy decisions. You will learn more about them in the process and they will grow professionally.

No one has all of the best answers. No one should be making all of the decisions, especially the everyday decisions. Allow subordinates a voice in the policy making process.

> "In all good
> things, reason
> should prevail."
> WILLIAM PENN

148

KNOW YOUR

COMPLETE

JOB DESCRIPTION

Always know the main goals and objectives of your superiors. If you are not sure, ask. Hard work does not do you much good when it is focused in the wrong direction. Stay abreast of where you are going and where you are leading others.

Make sure you read over your job description, if available, from time to time. Place additional tasking handed down to you in with your job description. Note who assigned the tasking and the date of the tasking. Add the duration of the tasking as appropriate.

Keep your job description up to date at all times.

> **Introduce one of your best people to the "boss at the top" from time to time.**

149

KNOW YOUR

STRENGTHS

& WEAKNESSES

This is not as easy as it may sound. Observe others around you and see how you compare to them. Know what you may be weak in when compared to others around you. Improve on your weak areas.

Work with someone more skilled than you in your weak areas. Learn and improve yourself.

Always try to have at least one exceptionally strong point. Become an expert in one aspect of your job. Concentrate your daily work effort in your expertise area while you are improving in other areas.

> **The effective leader stays in touch with others.**

150

BE HONEST AND

STRAIGHT-FORWARD

———

Be honest, straight-forward and professional when dealing with others in the work place. If you expect honesty and professionalism from others, they should be able to expect it from you.

People need to know where you stand on issues. Give them honest answers.

Knowledge
is
power.

151

EMPLOY

OVERALL & INDIVIDUAL

LEADERSHIP STYLE

When leading an organization, employ a basic overall leadership style. When dealing with individuals in that organization, use individualized leadership methods tailored to each person. That means different leadership traits work with different people.

Some individuals need only a gentle reminder while others require a more direct and forceful approach. You do not want to come down hard on someone who requires only a gentle nudge. *Always* start with and use the gentle approach toward each individual until that method proves unsuccessful.

When the boss calls for you, always take pen and paper with you.

152

INTEGRATE IMPROVEMENT

WITH

ORGANIZATION GOALS

Overall organization goals do not usually include internal improvements to individual units of the organization. However, you can make internal improvements that make you look good and improve effectiveness and efficiency at the same time.

Many people do not realize that they have an opportunity to write at least a part of their own performance appraisals. Look around your area of responsibility for areas that could use improvement. This is especially true when you first take over an organization. Find several areas that could be improved. Get these areas improved and then submit your accomplishments at performance appraisal time. The areas that require improvement should be added to your long-range priority check-list.

"Progress comes from the intelligent use of experience."
ELBERT HUBBARD

153

BE

PLEASANT

TO OTHERS

Make it a habit to be pleasant, cordial and courteous. Cheerfulness can be habit forming. *A good leader has a good personality.* A person with a bad personality cannot be an effective leader. Help make others feel happy and upbeat. Work with others for the common good of a team effort.

When you are not feeling well, or you are in a bad mood, stay away from others. Do not become a *grouch.*

> **Remember:**
> *LEADERS* lead people.
> *MANAGERS* manage things,
> events and activities.

154

PUT YOUR

BEST PEOPLE

IN STRATEGIC POSITIONS

Place your best people in strategic jobs and billets. The areas in your organization that are the most important to you (and your superior) should be where you place your most skilled, capable people. Re-design the "people structure" of your organization if necessary.

If you have a position that is *highly visible* to top management, always fill that position with someone who will project a proper professional image. Consider a person's knowledge, attitude, tact, courtesy, and dress when filling a *highly visible* position.

> **Positive reinforcement improves performance.**

155

DO NOT

STEREOTYPE

PEOPLE

Stereotyping occurs when someone attributes behaviors or attitudes to other people based on a particular group or category to which those people belong. Stereotyping leads to preconceived beliefs and ideas of other people. Treat each person as a unique, one-of-a-kind individual.

Each person can contribute to organization effectiveness and success. Failure to use someone's full skill and talent reduces your team's potential effectiveness and success. Do not let the stereotyping of people hinder your organization.

> The "daily routine"
> is work without a
> challenge; It breeds
> complacency.

156

SOLVE

PEOPLE'S

PERSONAL PROBLEMS

Many work-place problems stem from off-work sources. If you notice someone's performance or attitude take a nose dive, don't just automatically come down hard on the individual. Ask the person if outside or home situations are becoming a distraction. *Solve the problem, not the result of the problem.*

Helping people solve their personal problems *is* leadership. Sometimes leaders have to serve as mother, father, or big brother to others. The more effective you are at helping others solve their personal problems the more effective you become as a leader.

> "Leadership is the ability
> to get men to do what they
> don't want to do, and like it."
> HARRY S. TRUMAN

157

THREE

CATEGORIES

OF LEADERS

---

1) Those who **_MAKE_** things happen;

2) Those who **_WATCH_** things happen;

3) Those who **_WONDER_** what happened.

Stay in front and lead from the front. *Make* things happen, do not *watch* and *wonder*.

DEDICATION

Self-sacrificing devotion.

Commitment to something.

158

TAKE RESPONSIBILITY

FOR YOUR

ACTIONS

You may not always be right or correct. That is seldom as important as taking responsibility for your actions. Always accept responsibility for your actions, and the actions of the people working for you. *Accepting responsibility is the sign of a good leader.*

Your superior usually knows if you personally made a mistake or if it was someone working for you. There is no need for you to point your finger at a particular individual. The bottom line is that someone working for you made a mistake. Accept responsibility for the mistake, correct the mistake and move forward.

> **People
> want to believe they made
> a difference, that they contributed
> something someone else might not
> have contributed.**

159

ALWAYS

BE

LOYAL

Almost nothing is more treasured than *LOYALTY*: Loyalty to your organization, loyalty to your boss, loyalty to your subordinates. No one could ask for, or hope for, anything more than your loyalty. Practice loyalty on a daily basis. If you want others to be loyal to you, you should settle for no less of yourself.

You must give loyalty before you can receive it. Nurture loyalty and make it grow.

> **Most people will want to do a good job, if they are properly motivated.**

160

LEADERSHIP PRINCIPLES

THE "LEADER" VS. THE "DRIVER"

THE DRIVER	THE LEADER
Says "I"	Says "we"
Depends on own authority	Depends on good morale & esprit de corps
Inspires fear	Inspires enthusiasm
Throws weight around	Throws weight behind a mission
Fixes the blame for a breakdown	Fixes the breakdown
Rubs a mistake IN	Rubs a mistake OUT
Knows how it's done	Shows how it's done
Makes work drudgery	Makes work interesting

161

DON'T

KILL THE MESSENGER

WHEN YOU GET BAD NEWS

Do not be a part of the "*kill the messenger*" syndrome. This means that if someone reports bad news to you, do not take your displeasure out on that person ("messenger"). To do so is a good way to start closing down the lines of communication.

At the end of the day, ask yourself,
"Exactly what did I
accomplish
today."

162

SOMEONE

PUSHING YOU

MIGHT BE HELPING YOU

Does the boss push you to the limit from time to time? It might be because that person believes you have untapped potential that you do not know you have. Take this *"push"* as a personal challenge and a personal opportunity. You may surprise yourself at the results. Almost everyone needs an occasional external push.

> **Personally live up to whatever you expect of others.**

163

EXAMPLES

OF

BAD LEADERSHIP

━━━━

1) Don't do as I do, do as I say.

2) You are entitled to your opinion, I just don't want to hear it.

3) If I want your opinion, I'll give it to you.

4) Golden Rule: The one who has the gold makes the rules.

Few people would actually use the above sayings. Many people may do or say things that leave a listener with a similar impression. Be careful you are not one of them.

Just "getting through the day"
is not a prescription
for success.

164

HAVE NO

AMBIGUOUS

GOALS

Ambiguous goals and poor feedback can lead to confusion and frustration. This ultimately leads to poor performance in an organization. Goals should be described in detail. Goals should be written down for everyone's benefit. Feedback, negative or positive, should flow freely.

Explain an overall goal to your people. Next, go into some detail about individual parts of the goal. Ensure others know what part they have in accomplishing the goal. Do not forget to note the importance of the goal.

> **"The superior man is firm in the right way, not merely firm."**
> **CONFUCIUS**

165

PEOPLE

WANT TO UNDERSTAND

WHAT'S GOING ON

In today's world people not only want to know *WHAT'S* going on, they want to *UNDERSTAND* what is going on where they work. Keep your people up to date. The more informed people are the better they should be able to perform their jobs.

The more people know about the "big picture" of an organization the more they understand their individual overall role.

Understanding a task can be motivation in itself.

Everyone likes to feel appreciated.

166

INFORM SUPERIOR

OF IMPORTANT

MEETING INFORMATION

If you attend a meeting where some of the information presented could be of importance to your superior, orally pass that information along to him or her as soon after the meeting as possible. A more detailed written brief should follow if necessary.

A written brief to your superior should be typed to assure ease in reading. The date, time, and location should be stated along with the key participants. Key points made during the meeting should be connected to the people who made them.

> **Don't make threats or promises.**

167

THINK

BEFORE YOU

SPEAK

Engage brain before activating mouth. Remembering these few words would keep a lot of people out of trouble. Do not offer "off the cuff" advice. Do not make hasty decisions that have not been carefully thought out to conclusion.

Even casual comments can take on significant meaning. The higher up you go in an organization the more action will be taken in your behalf on a casual comment you make. Be careful with your comments, especially when you are around subordinates.

> **Most people**
> **are capable of doing more**
> **than their stated**
> **job description.**

168

PROVIDE NEW PERSONNEL

WITH ALL

IMPORTANT INFORMATION

Personally make sure that newly reporting personnel get a good first impression of your organization. Provide an overall "picture" of the operation and goals of the organization.

Explain how the individual fits into the organization. Cover all performance areas. Explain the chain-of-command structure. Ensure each individual reads all applicable printed material before being assigned duties (instructions, regulations, etc.).

As a minimum, introduce the new person to immediate superiors and subordinates before that person assumes any official duties and responsibilities.

Motivate yourself first.

169

NO ONE

SHOULD BE

INDISPENSABLE

An organization that cannot function properly when one person is missing is not properly structured or led. An effective leader should work himself or herself *OUT OF* a job, not *INTO* a job.

A good organization will function smoothly when anyone, especially the "boss," is not available.

The people working for you should be kept up to date on important matters. They should know your thoughts and ideas on key subjects, In short, when you are absent they should be in a position to make the decisions you would have made if you were there.

> Recognize and use
> the personal gifts
> of others.

170

ASSIGN

INDIVIDUAL RESPONSIBILITY

FOR EACH TASK

Always assign responsibility for a job or task to one person in a group, not the group at large. Explain to one person exactly what needs to be accomplished. Then, hold that one individual responsible for the task.

In a seniority system, always give the responsibility to the most senior person. You cannot effectively hold a group responsible for completing tasks.

Failure is an education in learning.

171

PRESENT

STRAIGHT-FORWARD

WRITTEN FACTS & INFORMATION

In written correspondence, do not try to impress the reader with big words or long, drawn out flowery sentences. Present the reader with straight-forward pertinent facts and information.

The reader should not have to wade through endless words looking for facts and information. The reader should look forward to reading your reports and information, not dreading it.

Be brief, be concise, and above all be accurate.

> "If I had no sense of humor,
> I would long ago have
> committed suicide."
> MAHATMA GANDHI

172

PHYSICAL EXERCISE

RELIEVES STRESS

Physical exercise does wonders for relieving daily stress and pressure. If your work is stressful, do some physical exercise to "unwind" at the end of a hard day. This can be in almost any form from jogging to walking to sporting activities.

Schedule your physical exercise and follow through on it. Ideally, you should do some strenuous exercise for 30-45 minutes 3-4 times a week, as directed by a physician.

Recognizing the successes and accomplishment of others is easy and inexpensive.

173

DECISIONS SHOULD BE MADE

AT LOWEST

COMPETENT LEVEL

Decisions and actions should be taken at the lowest competent level in any organization. When too many decisions are forwarded up the chain of command, superiors become bogged down in decision and detail. Also, the people who should have made the decision feel left out of the process.

Subordinates may have made the same decision as the superior. However, by not personally having a say in the decision, they may not be as enthusiastic about the outcome.

Remember the key word *competent.*

> **Ask open-ended questions and keep an open mind.**

174

FOLLOW-UP

AFTER ASSIGNING

TASKING

One key to success is to follow-up on all assignments. Follow-up is essential for several reasons. You need to determine if the work is being performed correctly and efficiently. Additionally, some people have a natural tendency to shy away from tough or irritating assignments.

Follow-up action keeps others aware that you are interested in the task.

> Ambition without drive and
> dedication is somewhat like
> a car without wheels.
> Neither ever get anywhere.

175

DON'T MAKE

SNAP

"NO" DECISIONS

When your superior asks you to do something, never respond with, "We cannot do that," or, "That cannot be done." Rather, say, "I will get right on it," or, "I will research that and get back to you." In this way you do not have to make a snap judgment that could be at least partially wrong. Investigate the matter carefully and proceed accordingly.

If a subordinate approaches you with a new idea, do not give an immediate *"no"* answer. Ask open-ended questions to ensure that you grasp the parameters of the idea. Tell the individual that you will give the matter your attention. Also inform the individual that you will get back to him or her with an answer.

> **Unrewarded acts**
> **can result in**
> **uninvolved people.**

176

FIND OUT

EVERYTHING

YOUR JOB ENTAILS

———

A leader's job or a manager's job can never be as clearly defined as a front-line operator. Do not expect to have every facet of your job written down in explicit detail.

In addition to whatever written guidelines and instructions you may have, ask your superiors about their expectations. Check with and observe your peers. See what they are doing and how they are doing it.

> ## TACT

The art of letting

someone have *your* way.

Diplomacy.

177

BE A "BUFFER"

BETWEEN BOSS

& SUBORDINATES

Be a "buffer" between your boss at the top and the people who work for you. Your boss will give you *GENERAL DIRECTIONS* on what is to be accomplished. You assign *SPECIFIC TASKS* to subordinates to help you accomplish your objectives.

To be a "buffer" is not to say to keep things from the superior, but to not pass along every complaint you hear from a subordinate. Pass along only what you think is important for the superior to know. Routine internal problems and complaints should remain internal.

> **IMPORTANT CORRESPONDENCE:**
> **Draft & wait a day.**
> **Review & wait a day.**
> **Finalize & forward.**

178

JOB PLACEMENT FOR

HARD CHARGERS

Difficult and demanding jobs should be given to your few "hard chargers." They need the challenge and you need the good performance in these areas.

These people want to get ahead the hard way--they want to earn it. See that they are given the opportunity.

Work to get these people promoted. Give it your personal attention.

"I can give you a six-word formula for success: Think things through, then follow through."
EDDIE RICKENBACKER

179

JOB PLACEMENT FOR

AVERAGE PERFORMERS

Routine tasks should be assigned to average workers. Do not put them in over their head, but do offer them jobs with some challenge and opportunity.

If someone shows potential for more difficult assignments, do not let it slip without notice.

Average performers should be promoted in an average amount of time.

Let
people know
their time and talent
is appreciated.

180

JOB PLACEMENT

FOR

BELOW AVERAGE PERFORMERS

Below average performers should be given more menial, repetitive tasks. This includes the daily routine tasks.

Close supervision is recommended for below average performers. **Do not** be satisfied with below average performers. *Work with this group to get improvement.*

Below average performers must be informed that it is *"shape up or ship out."*

> **Inject
> a little humor
> in the workplace
> from time to
> time.**

181

LEARN JOBS

& RESPONSIBILITIES

OF OTHERS

Know the scope and breadth of the jobs and duties of seniors and peers. You will get a better understanding of the overall operation of the organization. This will help you and your people work more cohesively with others in a total team effort.

By learning the jobs and responsibilities of superiors you are setting the stage for your promotion. Learn *WHAT* a superior is doing and *HOW* it is being done and you become qualified to fill that position. In the interim you become a more versatile person and a more valued member of the organization.

> **PARKINSON'S LAW:**
> **Work expands to**
> **meet the time**
> **allotted to it.**

182

PRAISE & RECOGNIZE

OTHERS

WHEN EARNED

Everyone likes to be recognized for good work. If you are not getting good work out of others it is your fault because you are their leader. If you are satisfied with the work of others, give them an occasional "pat on the back." Spread praise around liberally when it is earned.

If you have an individual who deserves promotion, give him or her extra work. If the individual is truly deserving of promotion you will receive excellent results. Praise that individual each time the extra work is accomplished and inform your superiors of the outstanding work. Soon you have one person receiving praise from everyone. Promotion is the logical next step.

TEAMWORK

Cooperative and

coordinated effort.

183

COOL DOWN BEFORE

DISCUSSING MISTAKES

Do not discuss a situation with someone when you are upset about a mistake he or she made. Cool down first and give the matter some consideration so that you can discuss the situation without an emotional outburst.

DISCUSS THE PROBLEM, NOT THE PERSON.

Train others.
Believe in and empower
them to do their work.

184

COMMON EXCUSES

FOR

FAILURE

———

1) I FORGOT

2) WAIT & ASK THE BOSS

3) THAT'S NOT MY JOB

4) THAT'S THE WAY WE HAVE ALWAYS DONE IT

5) NO ONE TOLD ME IT WAS IMPORTANT

Do not be caught using or relying on these excuses.

> "Indecision is the
> key to flexibility."
> In a leader, it is also
> a prescription for failure.

185

WITH

OPEN-DOOR POLICY

KEEP OPEN MIND

If you have an open-door policy, don't have a closed mind. An "*open-door*" policy means that you are personally available to anyone in your organization. If you subscribe to this policy, be sure you have an "*open mind.*"

One of the disadvantages of an open door policy is that it bypasses the normal "chain of command." Some matters brought to your attention probably could have, and should have, been resolved at a lower level.

If you use an open door policy, be careful not to let that policy become abused.

"He who has never learned to
obey, cannot be a
good leader."
ARISTOTLE

186

BE AN

ACTIVE

LISTENER

One of the most important skills that anyone can have, especially a leader, is to be a good listener. Being a good listener means to be an *ACTIVE LISTENER.*

An active listener keeps focused on the person speaking. If you are formulating a response while someone is talking, you are not *ACTIVELY LISTENING.* If you interrupt someone when they are talking, you are not *ACTIVELY LISTENING.*

When you are listening to someone speak, take notice of the body gestures. Body gestures are used by people to reinforce what they are saying.

> **If you do not have all the answers, keep asking questions.**

187

GIVE

SUBORDINATES

ROOM TO OPERATE

———

First, identify your best people. Second, give them authority. Third, give them room to operate. Do not be breathing down their neck every day to see how things are going. Give them the independence they need to do their job. *GIVE THEM OPERATING ROOM TO DO THEIR JOB.*

People who know how to do their job dislike anyone looking over their shoulder all of the time. Show your trust and confidence in your people by staying out of their way.

FORMULA FOR SUCCESS:
Keep an *ACTIVE MIND*.
Have a *FERTILE IMAGINATION*.

188

ONE TASK –

ONE

SUPERIOR

One subordinate should report to only one superior for a particular job or task. *One cannot serve two masters.*

Always follow this simple rule and make sure others working with you follow it.

A leader should groom his or her team to function smoothly in a single coordinated effort.

189

NURTURE RESPECT

AND

UNDERSTANDING

Mutual respect and understanding of others should be developed and nurtured by leaders. The ability to work together is a prerequisite for team effort and unity of purpose.

It is not enough to merely have respect for someone. You must demonstrate that respect in your actions and deeds.

Give others reasons to respect you and other members of your organization. More respect almost automatically means more understanding.

> **Everyone benefits from an *organized* management team. Everyone suffers from an *unorganized* management team.**

190

WHAT TO DO

IF YOU RECEIVE

CONFLICTING INSTRUCTIONS

If you receive a conflicting order, inform the person giving the order of your original orders. Then, carry out the second order if so directed. Next, inform the person who gave you the original order of the situation as soon as possible.

Follow the above simple guidelines and you should keep yourself out of trouble if these situations arise.

> "The best
> ideas are common
> property."
> LUCIUS ANNAEUS SENECA

191

DON'T "EXPECT"

ANYTHING YOU CAN'T

"INSPECT"

Periodically inspect the work of your subordinates. Stay up to date and make sure they stay on track. The earlier a mistake is caught, the less work required to correct it. Do not wait until a large job is completed before checking the work.

A periodic check on work should be a casual clue to others that you are interested in the outcome of the work. Demonstrating your interest in this fashion should make others pay attention to what they are doing.

People need to know their job as it relates to others in an organization.

192

SUBORDINATE DEVELOPMENT

IS YOUR

RESPONSIBILITY

It is your responsibility to ensure that all of your personnel are gaining the necessary knowledge and experience required for upward mobility. Give capable people a variety of jobs along with the necessary training.

Everyone should be given an opportunity to develop to their full potential. You are responsible for the professional training and development of everyone who works for you.

Always
have a back-up
plan of action
on important
jobs.

193

KNOW WHEN

TO DISCUSS

IMPORTANT ISSUES

Monday morning is the best time to discuss, or tackle, important issues. Friday afternoon is the worst time. Morning is better than afternoon; Monday is better than Friday.

**6P's
of management:
Proper Prior Planning
Prevents Poor Performance**

194

ENCOURAGE

CONTINUING

EDUCATION

Encourage all of your people to participate in off-work educational programs. The better educated and informed an individual becomes, the better that individual is to an organization. Make educational information available to everyone.

When someone completes an off-work educational class or program, announce it to others. This public recognition is another way of you showing your interest and support in continuing education.

ETHICAL

Conforming to accepted professional standards of conduct.

Principles of morality.

In accordance with rules and regulations.

195

LIMIT SIZE

OF WRITTEN

CORRESPONDENCE

Written correspondence should always be limited to 1 page whenever possible.

1 - Use short WORDS.

2 - Use short SENTENCES.

3 - Use short PARAGRAPHS.

4 - Place MOST IMPORTANT INFORMATION FIRST.

5 - Place DETAILS SECOND.

6 - Place OPINIONS/OPTIONS THIRD.

Informal acknowledgments raise spirits too.

196

PROVIDE EXPLICIT WRITTEN

INFORMATION TO SUBORDINATES

Every individual is entitled to be assigned explicit written instructions for his or her areas of responsibility. The jobs should be explained in some detail, as well as the expected performance standards. You cannot hold someone responsible for something you *think* they should know.

Each person should also be provided with the training and tools necessary to accomplish the tasks.

Failing to plan is
planning to fail.

197

PHYSICAL & MENTAL FITNESS

GO

HAND-IN-HAND

Establish and maintain a good personal physical fitness program. Mental and physical fitness go hand-in-hand.

People who exercise regularly to the point of breathing hard increase their overall blood flow circulation. Increased blood flow to the brain increases a person's ability to concentrate. The better you can concentrate, the better you can deal with the mental aspects of your work.

Strike up a *special* working relationship with a superior.

198

BE

OBSERVANT

Train yourself to identify areas of waste and inefficiency. Learn how to identify the people who are just going through the motions of doing a job. Then, take corrective action.

Observe what is being done and how it is being done. Allot a part of your time each day to going around your area of responsibility watching and observing others. This daily observation also keeps you up to date on the progress of ongoing work.

Be persuaded by someone's *LOGIC* and *PROOF*, not their enthusiasm.

199

HOW TO SPOT

GOOD & POOR

PERFORMERS

Need a quick way to determine your good and poor performers?

Good performers talk about opportunities, the future, and have a good attitude.

Poor performers complain about problems, workload, and have a bad attitude. A poor performer always finds fault with equipment or co-workers.

```
Do not discuss
sex, religion
or politics
at work.
```

200

WORK

WITH

PEER GROUP

———

Work closely and cohesively with your peer group. Do them a favor from time to time. They may return the favor when you need it most.

Peers are a good source of informal communications within an organization. Working with your peers helps you to stay in touch with overall organizational goals and schedules.

Working with peers promotes teamwork and enhances organizational communications. Ensure that the people working for you work closely with their peers.

> **"There is no security on this earth. Only opportunity."**
> **GENERAL DOUGLAS MACARTHUR**

201

WHAT DO YOU DO

WITH YOUR

TIME?

___

Take an average day at work and write down how much time you spend on the various facets of your job. Include time spent at your desk & time personally involved with others. Note how much time you spend on various projects and tasks, meetings, etc. At the end of the day, add up the time you spent.

Take the time you expended during the day and cross-check it against your highest priority jobs. Did you use your time working on the high-priority jobs? Did you spend ample time fulfilling your leadership responsibilities? Sitting behind a desk is not leadership. Did you spend too much of your time working on matters that could, and should, have been delegated to others? If most of your time was not spent on the high priority projects and in carrying out your leadership responsibilities, you need to revise your daily work schedule.

202

INVEST TIME

& EFFORT

IN OTHERS

Make a long term commitment to your people. Invest time and effort in their future and you invest in your future. Highly skilled people deliver highly skilled work. The more people know, the more they can contribute. Your efforts will be rewarded.

Training should be a mainstay in your organization. Invest time training others at every opportunity. The training can be formal or informal.

> "It is better to have
> one person working *WITH* you
> than to have three people
> working *FOR* you."
> DWIGHT D. EISENHOWER

203

CORRECT FALSE RUMORS

& GOSSIP

QUICKLY

Do not allow unfounded, false rumors or gossip to spread in your organization. There are always people who will spread false information or beliefs. False rumors adversely affect morale. You must stop these rumors at the earliest opportunity. There is no need to acknowledge rumors. Simply get the correct information out to your people.

A good two-way communication policy will prevent many rumors from being started.

When you do something, you should be proud enough about it to sign your name to it.

204

STAY

OUT OF

INTERNAL CONFLICTS

Anytime people work together there are going to be disagreements. Resolve disagreements among your people at the earliest opportunity. If disagreements or conflicts occur outside your area of responsibility, *DO NOT BECOME INVOLVED.*

Your priority should be to work harmoniously with everyone. Show others early and often that you are above becoming involved in internal conflicts and turmoil. This action is the sign of a good team player and a good leader.

Do not take sides in internal conflicts and disputes.

> TACT: The ability
> to describe others
> as they see themselves."
> ABRAHAM LINCOLN

205

YOU ARE THE MODEL

FOR THOSE

AROUND YOU

Your attitude, work habits, conduct and appearance set the pace for those who work around you. These traits should always be above reproach. Practice what you preach. You are the model for those around you.

If you want good teamwork, practice good teamwork. If you want others to work hard and produce top quality results, you lead the way.

To be a role model, think and act like a role model. Tell yourself, "If everyone did things as I do them, we would be an unbeatable team."

> **Nothing
> can take the
> place of
> experience.**

206

PERSONALLY

INFORM YOUR PEOPLE

ABOUT IMPORTANT ISSUES

Get all of your people together at a meeting and personally talk to them if you have something important to tell them. Do not rely on a few of your people to pass this important information along to everyone. This type of hand-me-down communication will lead to misunderstanding or misinterpretation, or both. If you have something you want everyone to know, tell them yourself.

Write down the highlights of your talk and distribute a memorandum. Restate the important parts of your talk. Do not leave anything to chance. Ensure that everyone gets the word. The memorandum will also serve as a reminder for people who did not take notes.

Recognition is a good motivator.

207

SATISFACTION

FOR A JOB

WELL DONE

———

Few things give a person more satisfaction than a job well done, especially when so noted by a superior. Tell an individual when he or she has done a good job. Tell the individual's co-workers.

Some people feel satisfied when they know that they have done a good job. Other people need feedback from a superior to reinforce that they have done a good job. In either case, when you are satisfied with a good job, tell people that you are satisfied. Make sure others receive recognition and satisfaction for a job well done.

> **Write to EXPRESS, not IMPRESS.**

208

GIVE YOURSELF

AN OCCASIONAL

ATTITUDE CHECK

A good leader should occasionally take a self-check on attitude and behavior. Consider your deeds, actions and words the past few days. How might others see you? Are you projecting the proper image?

The attitude and behavior of a leader will quickly spread throughout an organization. If you do not care about how something is done, others will not care. If you find yourself complaining, others will complain.

The proper mental attitude is a necessity for a leader. Give yourself an occasional *attitude check* to see how you are doing.

> **Failure to recognize someone's contributions to an organization is one of the most often voiced complaints by people.**

209

BE HONEST

& OBJECTIVE

WITH SUPERIORS

Offer a clear and honest answer when a superior asks your opinion on a subject. Do not make things seem better than they are, and do not hide part of the truth. Do not take sides on individual issues. Be prepared to offer options and alternatives.

Present facts and information to superiors without being too optimistic or pessimistic. State information matter-of-factly. Do not attempt to make jokes of bad news or a bad situation.

> "No power is strong enough to be lasting if it labors under the weight of fear."
> CICERO

210

SHOW INTEREST

IN

SUBORDINATES

Showing interest in, and attention to, a subordinate is one of the best ways to earn loyalty. Have an occasional one-on-one conversation. Ask people something about their personal interests. People work better when they get attention and know that you care about them.

If you work for someone who really cares about you as an individual, you are going to give your best effort for that person. Other people feel the same way.

INCENTIVE

Something that incites or has
a tendency to incite.

Incites to action.

Stimulating encouragement.

211

BUSY PEOPLE

FIND TIME

TO DO THINGS

There is an old saying, "If you want something done, give it to someone who does not have time to do it." People who are always busy get things accomplished. People who do not stay busy never seem to get anything accomplished.

Some people operate in high gear while others never get out of low gear. Both kinds of people are easy to spot.

Hard work and fun can be the same thing.

212

IF YOU

DON'T KNOW,

SAY SO

If you do not know the answer to a question respond with something along the line of, "I don't know, but I will find out and get back to you." Then, take that action. Do this with superiors and subordinates.

Do not give an answer simply to have an answer. If you do not know the answer, do some research.

People who even occasionally provide incorrect information or answers to questions soon lose their creditability. As a rule, anytime someone asks you a professional question and you do not know the answer, you should feel a need to know the correct answer. Find the correct answer even if it requires research.

> **Roll up your sleeves once in a while and join in with your subordinates.**

213

CONGRATULATE PEOPLE

IN PUBLIC SETTING

REGULARLY

Congratulate someone at least once a week for outstanding performance. If you have people working for you and at least one of them does not do something worthy of note on a weekly basis, you have a leadership problem that needs to be fixed immediately.

Congratulating someone in a public forum or setting is a form of *recognition*. Everyone has a need to be recognized. When you have people giving you their best effort, congratulate them in front of others.

> A
> leader
> should be visible
> and
> accessible.

214

DON'T MAKE DECISIONS

WHEN

TIRED OR UPSET

Never make a decision when you are tired or upset. You will usually come to regret it. When tired or upset, people tend to make *PERSONAL* decisions, not *PROFESSIONAL* decisions.

Even an occasional bad decision here and there adds up over time. It does not take too many bad, hasty, decisions to detract from organizational effectiveness and your abilities as a leader and a manager.

> Others around you have a great deal of knowledge in at least one subject. All you have to do to learn is to ask.

215

YOU WILL

WIN THE DAY

WITH PERSISTENCE

Never give up. Never let down. Never quit. That is persistence, to keep going when others quit. Take a different approach. Try something different. Do not be overcome by the short-term ups and downs. *PERSISTENCE WILL WIN THE DAY.*

The world is full of people who are not persistent. These people never achieve anything of significance. These people are referred to as *average people.* The world also has some people who achieve their lofty goals. These people are called *successful people.* All successful people have one thing in common--they are persistent.

> **It can take years of hard work to become an *overnight success.***

216

NO

FOUL LANGUAGE

IN WORKPLACE

Do not use foul language to describe something in everyday conversation. This shows a lack of professionalism and the ability to communicate effectively in everyday English. It also sets a bad standard in the workplace.

"The best morale exists when you never hear the word mentioned. When you hear a lot of talk about it, it's usually lousy."
GENERAL DWIGHT D. EISENHOWER

217

GIVE OTHERS

FREQUENT

COUNSELING & FEEDBACK

The only thing worse than a person how knows he or she is doing a bad job is a person who is doing a bad job, but thinks it is a good job. Most people want to do a good job. Provide frequent counseling and feedback to subordinates. Let them know how they are doing in their work.

Counseling and feedback should be given in a positive manner. Do not say something like, "Your performance is unsatisfactory." This immediately puts the person in a defensive posture. Any additional counseling will fall on deaf ears. Keep a positive tone and attitude when counseling someone.

**LEADERSHIP:
Sharing your vision
and courage to
inspire and motivate
others.**

218

PROVIDE SUBORDINATES

WITH

JOB DIVERSITY

Do not leave a person in the same job an inordinate amount of time. An important aspect of leadership is to develop subordinates professionally. Provide others with a variety of jobs and tasks. Doing the same daily routine eventually leads to a lack of enthusiasm among the more energetic people.

Your organization should be in a continuous state of training and learning. This action helps keep boredom from setting in as a result of completing the same job day after day. Job diversity offers challenge. Job diversity leads to a more effective and efficient operation.

> "Talkers
> are no good
> doers."
> WILLIAM SHAKESPEARE

219

GOOD VS. BAD LEADERSHIP

CHECK LIST

GOOD TRAITS	BAD TRAITS
*Truthful	*Untruthful
*Honest	*Dishonest
*Offers Hope	*Complains
*Fosters Trust	*Fosters Resentment
*Open-Minded	*Closed-Minded
*Gives Others Credit	*Takes All Credit
*Friendly	*Arrogant
*Specific Goals	*Ambiguous Goals
*Sets Good Example	*Sets Bad Example
*Requests	*Demands
*Takes Initiative	*Passes The Buck
*Makes Things Happen	*Waits For Things To Happen
*Provides Incentive	*Provides Dis-Incentive
*Condemns in Private	*Condemns in Public
*Develops Self-Confidence	*Tears Down Self-Confidence
*Works With People	*Flaunts Authority
*Offers Encouragement	*Offers Criticism
*Good Listener	*Poor Listener
*Delegates Authority	*Does Not Delegate

*Consistent Leadership	*Inconsistent Leadership
*Helps Others	*Helps Self
*Fair	*Unfair, Shows Favoritism
*Shows Respect	*Shows Disrespect
*Shows Enthusiasm	*Lacks Enthusiasm
*Asks Others	*Tells Others
*Works With People	*Works Through People
*Cares About Others	*Cares About Self
*Positive Feedback	*Negative Feedback
*Takes Action	*Promises Action
*Points Out Good Points	*Points Out Bad Points
*Develops Subordinates	*Does Not Develop Subordinates
*Good Role Model/Mentor	*Bad Role Model/ Mentor
*Sensitive	*Insensitive
*Stops Rumors	*Starts Rumors
*Interest In Others	*Self-Interest
*Sees Opportunities	*Sees Obstacles
*Attention To Detail	*Inattention To Detail

220

KEEP

SUBORDINATES

INFORMED

Failing to keep others informed and up-to-date is a problem suffered by almost every organization today. You probably receive routine, if not daily, briefings or information from your superior(s) in one area or another. How often do you pass this information along to your subordinates?

You must keep your subordinates informed of all schedules, upcoming events, the latest high priority jobs of your seniors, etc. Develop, and use, some method of prompt and efficient communications within your organization, from top to bottom.

Image is reality.

221

GIVE

OTHERS

CREDIT

When someone in your organization does something noteworthy, give them proper credit. Mention the deed or action at meetings, gatherings, etc.

Giving someone credit for something in front of your boss and the subordinate who deserves the credit is the most favorable form of credit. It demonstrates your honesty, integrity, and willingness to give credit where credit is due. The subordinate will remember you and the event for a long time.

> Take minor
> setbacks for
> what they are.

222

GET RID OF

THE "BAD APPLE"

All organizations occasionally face the misfortune of having a "*bad apple*" person in their midst. They can, and frequently do, spread dissatisfaction and discontent at every opportunity. Just one of these people can ruin an otherwise great organization.

Your job, as a leader, is to remove any *"bad apple"* influence as quickly and as painlessly as possible. Do not let one person disrupt your entire organization.

Attitude is everything.

223

BE CAREFUL

WHAT & HOW MANY

GOALS YOU SET

People who achieve goals tend to set and achieve new goals. People who fail to meet goals tend not to set or achieve new goals. Individuals must perceive goals as achievable to give it their best effort.

Be careful of the time and effort it takes to complete a specific goal, or set of goals. Sometimes new goals are accomplished at the expense of regular work or other projects. In this case, overall performance of an organization can remain the same, or actually decrease. Do not overload people or organizations with too many short-fused goals.

Goals are more likely to be achieved when the planner and the person or people who execute the goal jointly agree on the goal and the strategy. *Participation in goal setting influences commitment.*

224

PAINT

A

WORD PICTURE

───

When speaking to other people paint them a "**word picture.**" Allow them to mentally visualize what you are saying. Use words that are easy to understand by anyone and everyone listening to you. Provide examples if necessary.

Watch people's facial expressions when you are speaking. Their expression should be a clue as to whether or not they fully grasp what you are attempting to convey.

At conclusion, ask questions to determine if the painted word picture was successful.

> **Leaders should design organizations that solicit ideas and listens to others.**

225

STANDING TALL

AT AN

INTERVIEW BOARD

If you ever go in front of an interview board, check on the people who are conducting the interview. Find out who the people are. Know their likes and dislikes, and their areas of expertise.

Be yourself at the interview. Stay calm and casual and be business-like. Vary your eye contact when speaking, looking first to one person, then another, then another. Make each person think that you are talking to him or her personally. Do not use hand gestures.

Remember, all questions do not have *right* or *wrong* answers. Many questions are asked just to observe the way you react to the questions and to listen to you speak.

> **"Great souls have wills;**
> **feeble ones have only wishes."**
> **PROVERB**

226

DON'T MAKE

PHYSICAL CONTACT

WITH SUBORDINATES

It is a good rule of thumb not to make any out-of-the-ordinary physical contact with others at work. Any action of this sort could be misunderstood, either by the individual concerned or others in the immediate area.

Making physical contact with others can lead to accusations of *unprofessional conduct, fraternization, favoritism,* and similar uncomplimentary words. True or not, sometimes the stigma of the charge can linger on for some time afterwards.

> **There are
> no rules to
> regulate
> IMAGINATION.**

227

ALWAYS SHOW

PROPER RESPECT

FOR YOUR SUPERIORS

———

Get along with your superior(s). It is your responsibility, your duty. If necessary, it is your job to go out of your way to get along with your superior(s).

Everyone has a different personality, a little different way of doing things. You should come to expect this as normal.

You must have, and show, proper respect for someone in a position superior to yours. If you do not respect the person, you must still respect the position that person holds.

Failure to uphold proper respect for **any** superior lowers your standards as a professional and is disruptive to the good order and morale of your organization.

Be protective of subordinates.

228

BAD MANAGEMENT

KILLS

GOOD IDEAS

The only thing that makes a *good* idea work is a successful manager. Many good ideas fail because of bad management. To be a successful manager, you need to know if the *idea* or the *execution* was flawed.

If the idea was good but flawed, obtain feedback from others. Brainstorm with others to improve on the idea.

If the execution was bad, have a talk with the people involved. See if you can correct the management problem and implement the idea one more time.

You, as the leader, must find out why the idea failed.

> **KNOWLEDGE:**
> **The unending**
> **frontier.**

229

DON'T

RAISE YOUR VOICE

TO SUBORDINATES

A senior should *never* raise his or her voice to a subordinate. It will hurt the subordinate's ego and self-respect. This action will *not* be quickly forgotten or forgiven by the subordinate. Do not do anything to hurt someone's self-respect.

When you raise your voice you start to lose control--control of yourself and the situation. It is a lose-lose situation.

Any good leader can talk over a situation or correct a problem without raising his or her voice to another person.

> **Offer people the opportunity to grow and most of them will flourish.**

230

SHARE

YOUR

COURAGE

___

Share your courage. Keep apprehension and doubt to yourself. Do not weigh your people down with personal thoughts of despair or failure that will soon pass. Build them up with hope and courage.

There are many forms of personal courage. There is the "courage to stand on your convictions." Have the courage to stand alone when necessary. Have the courage to tackle difficult problems or situations.

Build on your confidence to have courage if necessary. Get your courage built up and share it with others.

```
Being
ANGRY
is
inefficient.
```

231

DO NOT

ACCEPT

AMATEUR WORK

——

There should be no place in your organization for amateurs or amateur workmanship. Always strive for maximum professionalism in yourself and others.

Your organization cannot be very successful doing amateur work. There is no personal or organizational pride in doing amateur work. Amateur work almost by definition means less than top grade, professional work. Do not accept amateur work.

> ## INITIATIVE

Energy or aptitude displayed
in initiation of action.

Ability to initiate action.

Do something without
being prompted.

232

DON'T EXPECT

INEXPERIENCED PEOPLE

TO MAKE RIGHT DECISIONS

Do not put an inexperienced person in a key job. You should not expect an inexperienced person to make the right decisions or take the correct actions.

Provide everyone with at least adequate training and experience *before* mistakes can be made, *not after* the mistakes are made.

If you want someone to make more experienced decisions, provide that person with more experience. Let that person have "hands on" experience under supervision. Give training and anything else required to get the experience they need.

> **INTIMIDATION has its limits.**

233

USE

YOUR

CHAIN OF COMMAND

———

Always stay within your *chain-of-command.* If you discuss important matters with someone above your immediate superior, inform that superior at the earliest opportunity. Do not let this fact get back to your superior through second-hand sources.

You would not be too happy if someone working for you went "over your head" to a superior about something. Your superior feels the same way.

> **Leadership**
> **is**
> **solving problems.**

234

WORK MORE HOURS

THAN

YOUR SUBORDINATES

You should be putting in more hours at work than anyone working for you. Do not expect others to be working for the goals and objectives of your organization when you do not or will not. If you want a full team effort, set the pace. You are, after all, the leader.

> "Reason and judgment are the qualities of a leader."
> TACITUS

235

DISSATISFACTION

IS THE *SYMPTOM*,

NOT THE *PROBLEM*

———

Dissatisfaction is not in itself a problem. It is a symptom of a problem. If someone is dissatisfied with only one aspect of his or her job, it may very well affect overall job performance. Seek out the real problem and then give it a solution.

Win the heart
and the body
will follow.

236

HOPE FOR THE BEST,

PLAN FOR

THE WORST

Hope for the best and plan for the worst. Always have an overall game plan. Be optimistic about it. Realize, however, that the more people involved in the plan the sooner something unexpected will happen. Remember the game plan is not the objective. The objective is to reach your objective--the reason for the game plan. Be adaptable. Anticipate that something may go wrong.

When something does go wrong, change your game plan, not your objective, deal with it and move ahead. Keep yourself and your people focused on end results, not an obsolete plan of action.

> **Know your assets
> and liabilities
> and plan accordingly.**

238

237

MAINTAIN AN

"ACTION"

TICKLER FILE

———

Maintain a tickler file of important dates. List reports, meetings, and any other occurring or recurring events or actions that require your time or attention in the future. Index cards (3"x5") are most helpful in maintaining a tickler file. You should never miss an important event, action or report because you forgot the date.

Planning and attention to detail help ensure success.

238

To be an effective leader, get a personal commitment from others. Say something like: "Can I count on you?" "I'm counting on you." Press their "*challenge*" button.

When important jobs and tasks come along, always get a personal commitment from the person doing the work or the person in charge of the work. When someone makes a personal commitment about something, chances are very good that that person will succeed.

> "Destiny is *not* a matter of *chance*, it is a matter of *choice*...it is a thing to be achieved."
> WILLIAM JENNINGS BRYAN

239

SEND A LETTER

TO THE

SPOUSE

When someone is promoted or earns a noteworthy award, send the spouse (or, mother or father if not married) an official letter noting that person's achievement. Indicate in the letter that dedication, hard work, and other appropriate information, were an important ingredient in earning the promotion or award. Thank the spouse for his or her support.

A letter takes very little time or money and it shows the organization's support of the individual and the family. The letter shows people that you care about the individual and the family.

> "People who fly into a rage always make a bad landing."
> WILL ROGERS

240

BREAK MAJOR TASKS

DOWN INTO

WORKABLE ELEMENTS

When major projects are at hand, get with others and break them down into integrated minor tasks. Use a flow chart if necessary. Break major tasks down into simple job elements. In this way they are easier to complete and easier to track.

If you give someone a monumental project, he or she may become overwhelmed by the task. Break it down into individual, workable parts. Take one step at a time. Set intermediate milestones for task completion.

> **Establish a professional working relationship with others for life.**

241

DESIRE & ABILITY

NEEDED IN

TASK ACCOMPLISHMENT

Watch whom you assign to complete a task. The most important elements in doing a good job are having the *DESIRE* and the *ABILITY* to do the job.

Proper training and experience can give someone the **ability** to do good work. Desire comes from inside a person. A leader must sometimes provide the proper external incentive in order to get the internal drive from an individual.

Providing the drive and ability to an individual are a part of fundamental leadership.

> **Volunteering shows your interest in, and your enthusiasm for, your work and your organization.**

242

DO NOT DISCUSS

YOUR PERCEPTIONS OF A

SUPERIOR'S MOTIVES

Do not discuss your perceptions of a superior's motives or actions with others. Such action shows lack of respect for leadership. You do not know the thoughts and concerns of others so you can only speculate, or guess, as to their reason or reasons for doing something.

Remember that while you are a *leader* to some, you are at the same time a *follower* to your superior.

Leadership is a two-letter
word ("WE"),
not a one-letter word ("I").

243

STAY FOCUSED

ON WHAT IS

IMPORTANT

Success starts with the ability to *STAY FOCUSED* on what is important. Successful people do not become weighted down in petty details or distracted by inconsequential matters.

Some people all too often do not remain properly focused on their top priority tasks because of minor distractions or "roadblocks." Successful leaders learn how to stay properly focused on their overall objectives and priorities.

ENTHUSIASM

To be inspired.

Strong excitement of feeling.

Something inspiring zeal or fervor.

Passion. Eagerness. Devotion.

244

MAINTAIN

A SENSE

OF HUMOR

Maintain a good sense of humor. Be willing to laugh at yourself. This helps you and those working with you keep an upbeat attitude. Turn a potential negative situation into a positive outlook. Putting a bright side to minor problems can help take away some of the frustrations of daily life.

Maintaining a sense of humor is a matter of **attitude**. If you take everything related to work as a serious matter, your attitude is out of balance. Learn to take serious matters seriously. Learn to take minor matters not so seriously.
In other words, keep a proper mental attitude and a sense of humor.

> "We confide in our strength, without boasting of it; we respect that of others, without fearing it."
> THOMAS JEFFERSON

245

TO BE RESPECTED

YOU MUST BE

PROFESSIONAL

To be respected as a professional you must act professional. It is hard to earn respect as a professional if you become involved in daily practical jokes in the workplace. Spreading rumors and gossip and using obscene language also detracts from professionalism.

Do not try to be "one of the guys" with the people working for you. You can be one of the guys with your peers.

Conduct yourself as a leader and a professional every hour of every day.

> "Never promise more than you can perform."
> PUBLILIUS SYRUS

246

MAKE YOURSELF

AVAILABLE

TO YOUR PEOPLE

The people working for you should be able to talk to you anytime they need personal and professional assistance or guidance. If they have a problem, even a perceived problem, their work will suffer until something is done to correct that problem.

Work stops if you are unavailable to make a decision or to provide clarification when needed. Always be available to your people.

If you are enthusiastic about a task, tell others why.

247

DEVELOP

GOOD PERSONAL CONTACTS

WITH PROFESSIONAL PEOPLE

Make it a point to meet and develop a good personal and professional working relationship with others within and outside your organization. Search out any person with a professional attitude who may be able to help you, now or in the future. This includes people in your peer group as well as people outside your immediate organization.

Let people know that if they ever need any assistance you are ready and willing to help them. They will return the favor. You cannot befriend too many truly professional people. Keep in at least periodic contact with these people even if you are transferred to another job or another location. You may be able to help each other in the future. It's a small world.

Develop these personal contacts for life.

248

BE PREPARED

WITH

PEN & PAPER

Always have pen and paper available on your desk or on your person. You never know when you are going to need them.

You might need to take notes during an important telephone call. A thought or idea might surface that will soon be gone forever if it is not written down quickly. Someone around you may say something that leads you to think of a new idea, a new way of doing something. You should always have pen and paper handy.

> Lead, follow,
> or get out of
> the way.

249

ABSOLUTE SAFETY

IN THE WORKPLACE

One of your most important jobs is to ensure that everyone working for you has a safe work environment. Do not leave it to others to inform you when there is a safety problem. Personally check for safety problems or violations in the workplace on a regular basis.

Tell everyone to inform you if they believe there is a safety problem, or a potential safety problem. These safety measures should extend to all people and all equipment, all the time.

> **Exchange ideas with other professional people on a regular basis.**

250

KNOW

EACH SUBORDINATE

INDIVIDUALLY

Your job is to fit the right person with the right job. Due to this you need to know each subordinate personally. Know the personal goals and desires of each person. *You need to know the talents and limitations of each subordinate.* You must determine what motivates the people working for you.

All of these things, and more, must be known before you can operate at maximum efficiency. Take the time to know your people.

> **Knowledge comes from action, not inaction.**

251

PROVIDE MAXIMUM

TRAINING & EDUCATION

OPPORTUNITIES

You should have a continuing training and education program in effect. It is impossible to give people too much training. Do not wait for someone to ask you for additional training. Technology is changing almost daily. New procedures, methods and practices are being developed all the time.

Your people should be leading the way, not lagging behind. For you to stay on top of your job, your subordinates must stay on top of their jobs.

"When you
have nothing
to say,
say nothing."
CHARLES CALEB COLTON

252

MAINTAIN

UP-TO-DATE

JOB DESCRIPTIONS

Adequate, up-to-date job descriptions are a necessity to hold someone accountable for job performance. People cannot perform effectively if they do not know what is expected of them.

At some interval, perhaps a couple of times a year, sit down individually with the people working for you and discuss job descriptions. Add and delete items as necessary. As your organization's goals and objectives change, so too should individual job descriptions.

> **Blaze a new trail.
> Do something no one
> has done before you.**

253

TRUST

YOUR

INSTINCTS

___

There will be times when you must make a decision without benefit of what you consider sufficient information. During these times, trust your instincts.

You have reached your present position because of good decisions made in the past. Consider the available information, consult with others, and then make your decision.

Find and study
character & actions
of a professional
role model.

254

MAKE

THE

RIGHT DECISION

Make decisions based on what is best for the organization. Decisions that may be the easiest for your or your people in the short run are usually not the best decisions for the organization in the long run. In the long run, decisions bad for the organization are bad for you.

Someone needs to think of the organization first. That person should always be you.

"Many receive advice, few profit by it."
PUBLILIUS SYRUS

255

YOU CAN'T LEAD

SITTING

BEHIND YOUR DESK

If you have a desk you probably spend a great deal of your time sitting behind it handling administrative affairs. Make it a point to get up from your desk several times a day and see for yourself how, and what, the rest of your organization is doing. See how it is functioning. Who is sitting around and who is doing the work?

Talk to your people and let them know that you are a part of their team. Keep your eyes and ears open. *YOU CAN'T LEAD SITTING BEHIND A DESK.*

> **To really motivate people offer rewards not punishment.**

256

PERSONAL

PRIDE

When you do something, you should be proud enough about it to sign your name to it. Think about it. No matter what you do, remind yourself that others will know it was your work, thought, or action. Take pride in everything you do. Make others around you proud of you.

Take pride in the way you dress. Take pride in the way and manner in which you command the use of the English language. Improve yourself and have pride in what you do every day.

Give everything your best effort and take pride in doing it.

> **What motivates one person may not motivate the next person.**

257

DON'T

MAKE

ENEMIES

Go out of your way to get along with peers and co-workers. You never know when you might need them. You should be able to work with other people from a professional standpoint even if you do not get along well with them personally.

Keep your personal opinions of people you do not like to yourself. Put yourself above personal verbal attacks on others. Do not lower your professional standards to the level of others who are less professional. Take the moral "high ground." It is hard to make enemies following these simple guidelines.

> "Success
> is a journey,
> not a
> destination."
> H.T. COLLARD

258

LEARN

FROM

OTHERS

———

Some people are always trying new ideas, new ways of doing things. Look around and see how others are doing in jobs similar to yours. When you find someone who is more effective or more efficient, find out what they are doing differently than you. Always be willing, and ready, to learn from others.

There is more than one right way to do something. Some ways are "*correct*" and more efficient; some ways are "*correct*" and less efficient. Be observant and *LEARN FROM OTHERS.*

**VERSATILITY:
The key to success.**

259

PAY

ATTENTION TO

DETAIL

The more individual details that are correct, the better chance the entire task will be correct. If you pay close attention to the little things, the bigger tasks often take care of themselves.

A leader should not *congregate* around the local "watering hole."

260

BE

CREATIVE

———

Search for better, more effective ways of doing old jobs. Work to improve on anything, everything. If you discover only one time-saving way to do something, you have increased efficiency. Several small creative ideas can greatly increase efficiency. Increased efficiency means you can be more effective at your job.

Creative people tend to rise to the top faster than others with otherwise equal talent. Everyone wants, and needs, creative people around them, especially the people at the top.

> You make the best
> impression doing the
> "every day"
> things right.

261

PASS ALONG

YOUR

KNOWLEDGE

Almost everything you know you learned from others. You are not the end user of that information. It is your responsibility to pass that knowledge on to the people who work for you. Keep the information process going.

The more information you pass along to others the more successful those people can become. If your people are successful, your organization will be successful.

Always encourage others to share their knowledge.

> If you don't push yourself,
> how do you know how far
> you can go?

262

ON-THE-JOB

LEADERSHIP

TRAINING

You can learn leadership concepts and values in a classroom or from a book. Develop your personal leadership skills by trial and error. You cannot learn how to bowl in a classroom or by reading a book. You cannot learn how to lead in a classroom or by reading a book. In both cases you have to practice it.

Learn from your mistakes, and from observing leadership traits and qualities, good or bad, from others around you.

> "A leader is a dealer in hope."
> NAPOLEON

263

MAINTAIN A

HIGH STANDARD

OF EXCELLENCE

Demand and expect only quality workmanship. When you do not get it, have it done again. If you demonstrate that you are willing to accept less than quality work, soon all you will be getting is less than quality work.

Show others that you are not going to be satisfied with anything less than a high standard of excellence. Your truly professional people expect this approach. Do not disappoint them.

Always maintain a high standard for the quality of work accomplished under your leadership.

Time can be your most valuable asset or your worst enemy. Manage it wisely.

264

WALK A MILE

IN ANOTHER

PERSON'S SHOES

―――――

If you really want to try to understand the people working for you, place yourself in their shoes. Reality is a matter of individual perception. See reality as others perceive it.

Imagine yourself actually working at specific work stations. What would you think of the working conditions? Imagine yourself with the income, social strata, influence and benefits of your subordinates.

Understanding other people, and their perception of reality, is a first step in knowing their likes and dislikes, and what motivates them.

> **Do not make promises you cannot keep.**

265

FIND TIME TO

TALK AND LISTEN

TO SUBORDINATES

Good leaders, no matter how busy, find time to talk with people and listen to their interests, problems and ideas.
Make it a point to say, "Hello, how are you doing today?" Or, "Are you having any problems that I can help you with today?" A few kind, friendly words will go a long way.

Most people can remember the last time they had a casual, friendly, one-on-one chat with their boss. It is not so much that they **try** to remember the chat as it is just thinking back on it as a pleasing experience. Have a friendly chat with your people.

PERSISTENCE

Act of being persistent.

Never quitting.

266

MEASURING

PERFORMANCE

STANDARDS

Be on the lookout for new ways to measure performance. Anytime someone's job description or content changes new performance standards may be needed. Standards of quality depend on how performance is measured. It is hard to put a price on quality.

Everyone needs to be able to measure their performance. Top management needs to measure individual performance and overall organizational performance and effectiveness. This is accomplished by establishing performance standards. Performance standards should be quantifiable whenever possible (time, percent, dollars, hours, etc.). Ensure the performance standards of people working for you are up-to-date.

> **Don't let a personal passion overcome your logic & good sense.**

267

ORGANIZATION

NOT FUNCTIONING

SMOOTHLY?

If your organization is not functioning smoothly as it should, ask yourself, "Are people doing the right job wrong, or are they doing the wrong job?" Reevaluate *WHAT* is being done, and then evaluate *HOW* it is being done.

People get into a habit of doing things in a certain way. Organizational goals and objectives change over time. Computers continue to change the workplace. Personnel changes take place at an ever increasing rate. Meanwhile, old tasks continue to be performed in the same old fashioned manner. Changes in what is being done and how it is being done should be made to keep pace with other events.

> **Rightly or wrongly, a person is first judged by his or her command of the English language.**

268

HELP STEM THE

PROFUSION OF

PAPERWORK

Organizations have a natural inclination to generate paperwork. If you want your organization to function more efficiently, eliminate as much time spent doing paperwork as possible. Each hour someone uses up processing paperwork is an hour lost in fulfilling the primary mission and tasks of your organization.

Today's most efficient organizations do not become bogged down in the paperwork shuffle.

Routinely ask yourself, and others, what reports, records, forms, etc. could be eliminated.

> Develop an insatiable appetite for success. Get a taste of it and you will want more.

269

ORGANIZE

FOR MISSION

ACCOMPLISHMENT

First determine the mission and tasks of your organization, then organize your personnel assets accordingly. Many organizations have become inefficient because their personnel structure did not change when their tasking was changed.

Use the following check-list to structure an up-to-date organization.

1 - Determine organization mission and tasks.
2 - Determine quality and quantity of personnel available.
3 - Structure the organization.
4 - Work on mission and tasks.
5 - Feedback to determine structure efficiency.
6 - Change structure based on feedback as necessary.

270

USE A

BULLETIN

BOARD

Use a bulletin board and keep it up to date. There are many advantages to using a bulletin board. Post the latest general information.

The following is a list of information that could be placed on a bulletin board.

1 - Latest information on organization mission and tasking.
2 - Names of people who made a significant contribution.
3 - Upcoming important events.
4 - Other information of general importance or interest.

There is no
substitute
for
good training.

271

SPECIALIZE

IN WHAT YOU

DO BEST

There are many aspects to any job; you need to be efficient in all areas. More importantly, you should specialize in one particular aspect of your job. Become the "resident expert" in one area of your work.

You want to be the person everyone turns to anytime something really important comes up in your area of expertise. The "boss" should automatically think of your name when these occasions arise.

"Either attempt it not,
or succeed."
OVID

272

ORGANIZE

YOUR

PAPERWORK

Organizing paperwork is an important aspect in any job. It is almost impossible to be efficient in your job if the paperwork is not processed effectively.

You should organize the flow and filing of paperwork in your office so that it is convenient and efficient for *you*. Do not worry about how the person before you processed and filed paperwork. Devise a system that works for *you*.

Go through all of the paperwork files, see if the system is efficient for the way you do business. Maintain a simple filing system. The less files the better. If you have several files with only one or two pieces of paper in them, find a way to combine the files.

Go through your files two or three times a year. Discard or combine files whenever possible.

273

ORGANIZE

YOUR

DESK

Your desk should be organized so that you can be efficient. The top of your desk should be maintained neat and orderly. Do not let books, files, etc. clutter the top of your desk. You may need an *"in"* basket and an *"out"* basket.

Do not leave personal or private paperwork on your desk unattended. Put it in a *"pending"* basket or put it in your desk.

If you have information you need close by, have a correctly cut piece of glass or plexiglass put on top of your desk. Place phone number listings and other appropriate information under the glass or plexiglass.

Keep an ample supply of administrative materials available (pens, pencils, paper clips, stapler, etc.).

274

Keep and maintain your *personal calendar*. A monthly calendar should prove very beneficial. Keep the current month and the next month in easy view. Look at it several times a day as a reminder.

List on your personal calendar all deadlines, upcoming events and activities, and any other information necessary to ensure that no deadlines are missed. Add and delete items as they come and go.

Be especially helpful
to others during times
of high stress.

275

LEADERSHIP

PERSONALITY

All good leaders have a well-developed personality. Which is to say that they are personable. To be a leader means that you must work with other people. A leader who is friendly, outgoing, and has a good sense of humor will accomplish much more than a leader who is an introvert, is unfriendly and lacks a sense of humor.

A good leader has a *likable personality*. People like being around a good leader.

Good leaders are not weighted down by personal egos or arrogance.

> Another word for
> *satisfaction*
> is
> *responsibility.*

276

DON'T BE

AFRAID TO

CHANGE

You cannot solve all of today's problems with yesterday's methods. Don't be afraid to change with the times. What worked for you in the past may not work for you today.

Ask others for constructive criticism. Ask yourself, too. Do not try to avoid or resist change. Some changes will be good and some will be bad. No changes will eventually be all bad.

Don't be afraid to experiment with change. Look forward to making a change from time to time. If a particular change does not work out, try something new. Keep trying to move forward and learn as you go. Above all, be certain of what you change and the outcome of that change.

> **A goal sets only a *minimum* expected result.**

277

JOIN A

PROFESSIONAL

ORGANIZATION

One of the best ways to learn or stay on top of your field or specialty is to join a professional organization.

You can also join a professional organization to learn or improve your skills. If you need to improve your speaking skills, join a public speaker's club. If you would like to improve your computer skills, join a computer club.

There is an almost limitless number of professional organizations. Join an organization that can improve your personal or professional skills.

> "Respect yourself
> and others will
> respect you."
> CONFUCIUS

278

PUBLIC

SPEAKING

———

When preparing for a public speech make notes that include the highlights of the information you intend to cover. Use these notes as a reference during the speech. Practice your speech in front of a mirror. Determine when to add emphasis to the speech either with tone variation or gestures.

Give the speech in front of someone you know and ask for suggestions. If possible, make a video recording of your practice speech and review it for possible improvements.

When presenting a speech, make eye contact with the audience. Look at the entire audience, in front, in back, to the left and to the right.

Keep the audience interested in your speech. Ask general questions that do not require a verbal response. This will compel the audience to think about what you are saying. Remain upbeat and speak with conviction.

At the conclusion of your speech, go over the high points again to reinforce what you covered.

APPENDIX

A

PERFORMANCE

APPRAISALS

All of the information in this appendix was taken from the book *THE DEFINITIVE PERFORMANCE WRITING GUIDE.*

See the back section of this book for information on how to purchase your personal copy of the nearly 500-page book, *THE DEFINITIVE PERFORMANCE WRITING GUIDE.*

PERFORMANCE

APPRAISAL

PREPARATION CHECK-LIST

1. Performance appraisals should be handled discretely. They should be worked on in private.

2. Copies of previous appraisals should be reviewed if possible.

3. People being evaluated in comparable or competitive categories should be evaluated at the same time. This will facilitate comparative grading.

4. Try not to gravitate toward either a gratuitously high or rigidly severe policy of evaluating others.

5. Exercise care to evaluate objectively. Avoid any tendency that might allow general impressions, a single incident, or a particular trait, characteristic, or quality to influence the appraisal unduly.

6. Before you begin to write, check over any available information and determine an overall performance placement of the person being evaluated (e.g. HIGHLY FAVORABLE, FAVORABLE, or UNFAVORABLE).

When this determination has been made, write a performance appraisal that will support and justify your position.

7. If grading or ranking marks are assigned, and they are significantly higher or lower than previous appraisals, a reason for the change might need to be included in the write-up.

8. Remember, words in a performance appraisal are both valuable and dangerous tools. Choose them carefully.

9. Before submitting a smooth performance appraisal, analyze the narrative to make sure that what is meant to be written, is in fact, actually being written. Give careful thought not only to the words you want to use, but also what the words will mean to others.

10. When the performance appraisal is finished, review it to ensure that:

   a. Any grading or ranking marks agree with the narrative.

   b. Any increasing or decreasing trend in performance is correctly conveyed.

11. Guard against repetitive phraseology on subsequent performance appraisals.. Do not write the same thing time after time.

PERFORMANCE APPRAISAL

"DO"

CHECK-LIST

1. DO submit performance appraisals on time and in the correct format.

2. DO write on HOW someone contributed above or below what is normally expected.

3. DO write to express, NOT impress.

4. DO be fair, honest, and objective.

5. DO write using hard, pertinent facts, not "faint praises" without substance.

PERFORMANCE APPRAISAL

"DON'T"

CHECK LIST

1. DON'T assign grades or marks that are inconsistent with a narrative write-up.

2. DON'T include minor, isolated, or insignificant imperfections that do not affect performance. A person does not have to be perfect to receive a good appraisal.

3. DON'T use "glittering generalities" that go on and on without saying anything useful.

4. DON'T use long words when shorter words will do just as well.

5. DON'T be verbose or redundant by writing the same thing over and over again. Cover an area of subject adequately and move on to another subject.

6. DON'T start every sentence with the person's name. Reading becomes sluggish and boring, and shows a lack of attention or ability on the part of the drafter.

7. DON'T evaluate someone's performance based on a comparison of another person whose job requirements are different.

8. DON'T restrict your evaluation of a new person to the amount of skill or knowledge they have acquired up to a particular point in time. Consider the amount of time it has taken that person to learn the skill or knowledge (e.g., learns at a faster than normal pace, slower than normal pace, etc.).

CHOOSE

YOUR WORDS

CAREFULLY

Words are both valuable and dangerous tools. Choose them carefully. Review the following:

POTENTIAL CAPACITY ABILITY
To indicate that an individual has one of these qualities without the proper support words is not saying anything useful. A person can have POTENTIAL, CAPACITY, or ABILITY and yet accomplish nothing. If you use words such as these, go on to write how these qualities were demonstrated.

TRIES STRIVES ATTEMPTS
Someone can TRY, STRIVE, or ATTEMPT to do something without accomplishing anything. As above, note how these qualities were demonstrated.

ACCEPTS ASSIGNED
Simply ACCEPTING a job does not show initiative. Performing an ASSIGNED job does not show initiative.

NORMALLY GENERALLY USUALLY
These words mean less than always.

AVERAGE ABOVE AVERAGE
EXCELLENT SUPERIOR
These words have come to have *"canned"* meanings. ABOVE AVERAGE is generally assumed to mean less than EXCELLENT. And, EXCELLENT is good, but it is less than SUPERIOR. If you intend to place someone's performance in one of these categories, be sure to choose the correct word(s).

AGGRESSIVE
Be careful how you use this one. If the word AGGRESSIVE is linked to a person's personality, it may be understood by the reader that the person is overbearing. But, to write that a person is JOB AGGRESSIVE gives the reader a completely different impression.

PERFORMANCE APPRAISAL

"BULLET PHRASE"

STATEMENTS

———

What is a "bullet phrase?" A bullet phrase is a statement that may or may not have a subject, object, or verb.

Bullet phrases are straightforward, matter-of-fact statements. Bullet phrases serve to reduce the amount of space required to make a statement. Thus, using bullet phrases allows more material to be covered in the same space, or the same amount of material to be covered in less space than using formal sentence structure.

The following pages list some sample words and "bullets" to use when drafting performance appraisals. The bullets can be turned into complete sentences if necessary.

SUPERIOR PERFORMANCE

"BULLETS"

2-WORDS

- RELENTLESS DEDICATION
- BOUNDLESS ABILITY
- EXCEPTIONAL RESULTS
- ULTIMATE PROFESSIONAL
- STRONGLY MOTIVATED
- TIRELESS DEDICATION
- UNRELENTING EFFORT
- INEXHAUSTIBLE ENERGY
- WITHOUT EQUAL
- HARD CHARGER
- BANNER PERFORMER
- HIGHLY RESPECTED
- OUTSTANDING WORKER
- SELF SACRIFICING
- GREAT ENTHUSIASM
- UNLIMITED POTENTIAL
- STELLAR PERFORMER
- METICULOUSLY ACCURATE
- INSATIABLE CURIOSITY
- FLAWLESS PERFORMANCE
- SIGNIFICANT CONTRIBUTIONS
- INDUSTRIOUS NATURE
- EXCEPTIONAL TALENT

SUPERIOR PERFORMANCE

"BULLETS"

3-WORDS

- ALWAYS GIVES 100%
- EXCEEDS HIGHEST EXPECTATIONS
- EXCEPTIONALLY WELL ORGANIZED
- PERSEVERING AND ENDURING
- METICULOUS IN MANNER
- GREAT PERSONAL INDUSTRY
- RESOLUTE IN ACTION
- SOLID PROFESSIONAL COMPETENCE
- RESULTS ALWAYS IMPRESSIVE
- PROFICIENT AND INDUSTRIOUS
- ADDS EXTRA DIMENSION
- BENCHMARK OF EXCELLENCE
- THRIVES ON DIVERSITY
- CAPTURES THE IMAGINATION
- REACHES NEW HEIGHTS
- DECISIVE, ACTION ORIENTED
- ORGANIZED AND INDUSTRIOUS
- UNCOMMON PROFESSIONAL INSIGHT
- MAINTAINS HIGHEST STANDARDS
- CONSISTENTLY SUPERIOR RESULTS
- SOUND PROFESSIONAL JUDGMENT
- ALWAYS HIGHLY MOTIVATED
- RICH TECHNICAL EXPERTISE

SUPERIOR PERFORMANCE

"BULLETS"

4-WORDS

- SUCCESSFULLY MEETS ANY CHALLENGE
- REPUTATION FOR DEPENDABLE RESULTS
- INTENSE DESIRE TO SUCCEED
- ROUTINELY RESOLVES DIFFICULT PROBLEMS
- METICULOUS ATTENTION TO DETAIL
- TOTAL COMMITMENT TO JOB
- RELENTLESS ENERGY AND DRIVE
- INGRAINED PURSUIT OF EXCELLENCE
- CREATIVE AND DECISIVE NATURE
- ENDLESS ZEAL AND ENTHUSIASM
- UTMOST DEGREE OF ACCURACY
- RESPONSIVE TO ALL TASKING
- ADMIRABLE COURAGE OF CONVICTION
- ALERT, QUICK AND RESPONSIVE
- UNLIMITED ABILITY AND POTENTIAL
- GREAT STRENGTH OF CHARACTER
- SUPERIOR KNOWLEDGE OF JOB
- REMARKABLE ABILITY TO ADAPT
- VERY QUICK AND THOROUGH
- IGNITES ENTHUSIASM OF OTHERS
- TOTALLY COMMITTED TO EXCELLENCE
- ACTS DECISIVELY UNDER PRESSURE

ABOVE AVERAGE PERFORMANCE

"BULLETS"

2-WORDS

- POSITIVE RESULTS
- PRACTICAL INDIVIDUAL
- SINCERE EFFORT
- ALWAYS BUSY
- GOOD DETERMINATION
- QUALITY WORKER
- ENERGETIC PERSONALITY
- TRIES HARD
- PERFORMS WELL
- FAITHFUL WORKER
- POSITIVE OUTLOOK
- LIKES CHALLENGES
- FAVORABLE RECORD
- EARNEST PERFORMER
- DEVELOPING QUICKLY
- EXPERIENCED WORKER
- KEEPS BUSY
- CONFIDENT INDIVIDUAL
- STAYS ORGANIZED
- PRUDENT ACTION
- POSITIVE ATTITUDE
- MAKES CONTRIBUTIONS

ABOVE AVERAGE PERFORMANCE

"BULLETS"

3-WORDS

- EFFECTIVE AND EFFICIENT
- ALWAYS ACCURATE WORK
- TAKES PROPER ACTION
- AGGRESSIVE WORK PERFORMANCE
- A COMPETITIVE SPIRIT
- DEDICATED TO WORK
- EXCELS AT JOB
- SHOWS GOOD LOYALTY
- DELIBERATE WORK HABITS
- COOPERATIVE AND HELPFUL
- PURSUES TASKS DILIGENTLY
- GIVES CREDIBLE PERFORMANCE
- ENHANCES TEAM SPIRIT
- SKILLFULLY ATTACKS WORK
- TAKES DESIRED ACTIONS
- CONFIDENT OF ABILITIES
- PROMPT IN RESPONSE
- STRIVES FOR SUCCESS
- USES TIME WISELY
- PROMPT AND RESPONSIVE
- HARD WORKING INDIVIDUAL
- ALWAYS GOOD RESULTS
- A THOROUGH WORKER

ABOVE AVERAGE PERFORMANCE

"BULLETS"

4-WORDS

- ACTS CORRECTLY UNDER PRESSURE
- GOOD SENSE OF RESPONSIBILITY
- STAYS PREPARED AND READY
- ALWAYS ENERGETIC AND HELPFUL
- PLANS CAREFULLY AND WISELY
- PROMPT, PROPER IN ACTION
- TAKES PRIDE IN WORK
- GOOD CAPACITY FOR GROWTH
- POSITIVE OUTLOOK AND ATTITUDE
- COMPETENT IN MOST SITUATIONS
- FLEXIBLE, ABLE TO ADAPT
- ALWAYS DOES FAVORABLE WORK
- LIKES TO STAY BUSY
- WELL SKILLED IN JOB
- PUTS FORTH QUALITY EFFORT
- TAKES PRIDE IN WORK
- GOOD LEVEL OF RELIABILITY
- SHOWS ATTENTION TO DETAIL
- HIGH DEGREE OF ACCURACY
- KEEN INTEREST IN WORK
- COPES WITH DIFFICULT SITUATIONS
- WELL TRAINED AND PRODUCTIVE

AVERAGE PERFORMANCE

"BULLETS"

2-WORDS

- SINCERE EFFORT
- ADEQUATE PERFORMANCE
- TECHNICALLY CAPABLE
- HAS DETERMINATION
- TRIES HARD
- GOOD WORKER
- KEEPS ORGANIZED
- POSITIVE ATTITUDE
- ALWAYS PUNCTUAL
- RELIABLE EFFORT
- AVERAGE WORK
- ACCEPTABLE PERFORMANCE
- CAPABLE INDIVIDUAL
- COMPETENT JOB
- MODERATELY SUCCESSFUL
- DEPENDABLE PERFORMANCE
- ABLE WORKER
- STEADY WORKER
- ACCEPTS RESPONSIBILITY
- SUPPORTS RULES
- TYPICALLY EFFECTIVE
- ASSISTS OTHERS
- AVERAGE TALENT

AVERAGE PERFORMANCE

"BULLETS"

3-WORDS

- GOOD WORK HABITS
- DOES ACCURATE WORK
- ADEQUATELY COMPLETES WORK
- ADHERES TO RULES
- USUALLY ERROR-FREE WORK
- RELIABLE WORK HABITS
- GIVES DESIRED EFFORT
- COOPERATIVE AND HELPFUL
- DELIBERATE WORK HABITS
- HAS AMPLE COMPETENCE
- DOES HELPFUL WORK
- CONSCIENTIOUS ABOUT JOB
- CAREFUL ABOUT DETAIL
- NEAT AND ORDERLY
- MEETS JOB REQUIREMENTS
- GIVES ROUTINE EFFORT
- SHOWS REASONABLE EFFORT
- INTERESTED IN JOB
- TAKES DESIRED ACTIONS
- PUNCTUAL FOR WORK
- FOLLOWS DIRECTION WELL
- WILLING TO LEARN

AVERAGE PERFORMANCE

"BULLETS"

4-WORDS

- GOOD SENSE OF RESPONSIBILITY
- WILLING TO HELP OTHERS
- PLEASANT TO WORK WITH
- ORDERLY AND ORGANIZED EFFORT
- ABIDES BY THE RULES
- ADAPTS TO CHANGING REQUIREMENTS
- CONTRIBUTES TO TEAM EFFORT
- WELL SKILLED IN JOB
- MOST WORK IS ACCEPTABLE
- PERFORMS ROUTINE JOBS WELL
- EASY TO WORK WITH
- HAS INTEREST IN WORK
- TRIES TO IMPROVE SELF
- CAPABLE AND EFFICIENT EFFORT
- GOOD DEDICATION TO JOB
- SUITABLE FOR MOST JOBS
- WORKS WELL WITH SUPERVISION
- CONFORMS TO JOB REQUIREMENTS
- GOOD RECORD OF PERFORMANCE
- SEEKS SOLUTIONS TO PROBLEMS
- OBEYS POLICY AND PROCEDURE
- FAIR AMOUNT OF TALENT

BELOW AVERAGE PERFORMANCE

"BULLETS"

2-WORDS

- MEDIOCRE PERFORMER
- EASILY DISTRACTED
- MINIMUM CONTRIBUTION
- LIMITED POTENTIAL
- INCONSISTENT WORKER
- LITTLE PROGRESS
- LACKS PERSISTENCE
- REQUIRES SUPERVISION
- UNIMPRESSIVE WORK
- OVERBEARING PERFECTIONIST
- MARGINAL WORK
- LACKADAISICAL ATTITUDE
- COMPLACENT PERFORMANCE
- LETHARGIC BEHAVIOR
- NONCHALANT ATTITUDE
- ERRATIC PERFORMANCE
- MEAGER PRODUCTIVENESS
- SQUANDERS TIME
- SHORTSIGHTED EFFORT
- SUBSTANDARD PERFORMANCE
- UNPRODUCTIVE INDIVIDUAL
- UNFINISHED WORK

BELOW AVERAGE PERFORMANCE

"BULLETS"

3-WORDS

- BECOMES EASILY DISTRACTED
- CONSISTENT MARGINAL PERFORMANCE
- SLOW, PLODDING WORK
- EXERTS MINIMUM EFFORT
- REQUIRES REGULAR REMINDERS
- BECOMES EASILY FRUSTRATED
- HABITUAL IRREGULAR WORK
- SLOW AND METHODICAL
- SHOWS LITTLE EFFORT
- SLOW TO ACT
- WORK NOT TIMELY
- LIMITED GROWTH POTENTIAL
- NOT VERY EFFICIENT
- LACKS STEADFAST DEDICATION
- CANNOT STAY MOTIVATED
- WORK IS INCONSISTENT
- COMMITS MINOR INFRACTIONS
- INEXACT IN DETAIL
- PALTRY WORK OUTPUT
- INATTENTION TO DETAIL
- RESULTS MOSTLY INSIGNIFICANT
- WORK MOSTLY COMMONPLACE

BELOW AVERAGE PERFORMANCE

"BULLETS"

4-WORDS

- PUTS FORTH MINIMUM EFFORT
- TOLERANT OF MEDIOCRE EFFORT
- TENDS TO BE TROUBLESOME
- SLOW WORKER AT BEST
- ALL DEADLINES NOT MET
- SHIRKS RESPONSIBILITY IF POSSIBLE
- UNPREDICTABLE ATTENTION TO DETAIL
- TIRES OF WORK EASILY
- FAILS TO MEET EXPECTATIONS
- NOT CAREFUL ABOUT WORK
- LACKS AGGRESSIVE WORK HABITS
- HAS LAPSES OF MEMORY
- MAKES ERRORS IN JUDGMENT
- ENJOYS BEING NONCONFORMIST
- HAS TENDENCY TO FORGET
- SOME JOBS COMPLETED INACCURATELY
- EXHIBITS LACK OF ENTHUSIASM
- TRIES HARD, ACHIEVES LITTLE
- WORK OF INFERIOR QUALITY
- BECOMES CONFUSED ABOUT JOB
- NOT DEDICATED TO WORK
- JOB NOT FIRST PRIORITY

UNSATISFACTORY PERFORMANCE

"BULLETS"

2-WORDS

- AVOIDS RESPONSIBILITY
- NOT MANAGEABLE
- INFERIOR WORK
- PROFESSIONALLY STAGNANT
- IMPOTENT WORK
- PATHETIC PERFORMANCE
- MISUSES POSITION
- LOSES CONTROL
- LACKS IMAGINATION
- TOTALLY UNCONCERNED
- COMPLETELY HELPLESS
- IMPEDES PROGRESS
- SHIRKS RESPONSIBILITY
- WASTED OPPORTUNITIES
- BLATANT NEGLIGENCE
- DISRUPTIVE INFLUENCE
- UNDERMINES MORALE
- IGNORES DIRECTION
- CREATES PROBLEMS
- DEFEATIST ATTITUDE
- NOT TRUSTWORTHY
- LACKS SELF-DISCIPLINE
- SLOPPY WORKMANSHIP

UNSATISFACTORY PERFORMANCE

"BULLETS"

3-WORDS

- CONTINUOUS POOR ATTITUDE
- HABITUALLY FLOUTS AUTHORITY
- EFFORTS ROUTINELY FUTILE
- UNSATISFACTORY WORK RESULTS
- DEPLORABLE WORK ETHICS
- REQUIRES CONSTANT SUPERVISION
- ADVERSELY AFFECTS MORALE
- A COMPLETE DISAPPOINTMENT
- NO FUTURE POTENTIAL
- VIOLATES THE RULES
- FREQUENT MISCONDUCT PROBLEMS
- NEGLECTFUL AND INCOMPETENT
- ROUTINELY OBSTRUCTS PROGRESS
- MAKES FREQUENT MISJUDGMENTS
- INCONSIDERATE OF OTHERS
- ROUTINELY FAULTY WORK
- INCOMPETENT AT JOB
- UNPREDICTABLE WORK HABITS
- PLAGUED BY INDECISION
- UNWILLING TO CONFORM
- DELIBERATELY REFUSES DIRECTION
- DISCOURAGES TEAM UNITY
- MISREPRESENTS THE FACTS

UNSATISFACTORY PERFORMANCE

"BULLETS"

4-WORDS

- ILLOGICAL PERFORMANCE AND ACTIONS
- IDEALISTIC TO A FAULT
- FLAGRANT VIOLATIONS OF DIRECTIONS
- COMMON ERRORS IN JUDGMENT
- FREQUENTLY DEVIATES FROM STANDARDS
- UNCERTAIN, INDECISIVE IN ACTION
- EFFORTS FREQUENTLY PROVE FRUITLESS
- IGNORES DIRECTION AND GUIDANCE
- EXHIBITS LACK OF DESIRE
- SUBJECT TO DAILY FAILURE
- LACKS PROPER MENTAL DISCIPLINE
- UNWILLING TO OBEY DIRECTION
- PREJUDICIAL TO GOOD ORDER
- DETRIMENTAL TO TEAM SPIRIT
- OBVIOUS LACK OF MOTIVATION
- NOT RECEPTIVE TO COUNSELING
- A BURDEN TO OTHERS
- TOO MANY PETTY MISTAKES
- INTERRUPTS WORK OF OTHERS
- WORK RIDDLED WITH DEFECTS
- LACK OF PERSONAL CONVICTION
- SERIOUSLY LACKING IN INITIATIVE
- WILL BOTCH ANY JOB

NAVY BOOKS & PRODUCTS

The Naval Officer's Manual (600+ pages) (Hard Cover) $25.95
Drafting O&R manuals, SOPs, Job Descriptions, Correspondence, Personal
Awards. Leadership principles & concepts. Navy ships, aircraft, & weapons
systems. Navy vocabulary. Much more.

The Chief Petty Officer's Manual (548 pages) (Hard Cover) $25.95
E-7/8/9 Selection Boards. LDO/CWO Selection Boards. Leadership
Management, Organization, Retirement Ceremonies, Evals, SOPs, Job
Descriptions, Navy vocabulary and Acronyms, Correspondence, Ships, Aircraft.
More.

The Navy Petty Officer's Manual (450+ pages) (Hard Cover) $25.95
Preparing for exams, Leadership, Watch Bill Preparation, Awards, Types of
Duty, Uniforms, evaluations, writing/speaking, repair/maintenance, LDO/CWO
programs. More.

U.S. Navy Dictionary: Terms, Abbreviations, & Acronyms (250+ pages)
(Hard Cover) $25.95
Comprehensive reference book filled with thousands of basic and technical terms
with accurate definitions. Plus, abbreviations & acronyms defined for everyday
use.

Enlisted Surface Warfare Specialist (ESWS) Study Guide (300+ pages) $27.95
Complete, in-depth discussion & answers for ESWS PQS. Pictures &
illustrations. Greatly reduces time required to become ESWS qualified. Serves as
ready-reference for qualification board members.
Enlisted Surface Warfare Specialist (ESWS) Audio Tapes (Six 90-minute
Q&A tapes) $29.95
Highlights of the ESWS book provided in this set of audio tapes in form of
questions & answers.

Enlisted Aviation Warfare Specialist (EAWS) Study Guide (300+ pages) $27.95
1,000+ detailed and in-depth answers to EAWS qualification. Pictures &
illustrations. Greatly reduces time required to become EAWS qualified. Serves
as ready-reference for qualification board members.
Enlisted Aviation Warfare Specialist (EAWS) Audio Tapes (Six 90-minute
Q&A tapes) $29.95
Highlights of the EAWS book provided in this set of audio tapes in form of
questions & answers.

NAVY BOOKS & PRODUCTS (Cont.)

Navy-Wide Exam Advancement Guide for E-4 Thru E-7 (336 pages) $24.95
NOT FOR ANY PARTICULAR RATING. Written by ex-exam writer. Explains
how to improve your test score on any Navy-wide exam. Includes preparation,
exam strategy, how to spot correct & incorrect answers. **Bonus**: 1200 Q&A
section covering Military Leadership portion of all Navy exams. More.

Navy Military Leadership Audio Tapes for E-4 & E-5 (3 90 minute Q&A
tapes) $25.95
Navy Military Leadership Audio Tapes for E-6 & E-7 (3 90-minute Q&A
tapes) $25.95

Study Guide for Advancement (*Various USN Ratings*) (books) $29.95
Study Guide for Advancement (*Various USN Ratings*) (audio tape sets) $ 33.95

Navy Trivia Quiz Book $10.95. 1,000 Q&A on Navy trivia/history items.

COMPUTER CLIP ART GRAPHICS SETS

ALL CLIP ART ON IBM 3.5" DISKS, 3-5 DISKS PER SET.
All Clip Art in ".PCX" FORMAT
1-SET $49.95   2-SETS @ $44.95 each
3-SETS @ $39.95 each,   4 or more sets @ $34.94 each
- **AIRCRAFT CLIP ART**
- **MILITARY GRAPHICS COLLECTION**
- **AIR FORCE CLIP ART**
- **ARMY CLIP ART**
- **MARINE CORPS CLIP ART**
- **COAST GUARD OFFICER CLIP ART**
- **COAST GUARD ENLISTED CLIP ART**
- **NAVY OFFICER CLIP ART**
- **NAVY ENLISTED CLIP ART**
- **NAVY SHIP GRAPHICS CLIP ART**

SHIPPING: Add $3.00 Per Item for Regular Mail, or $5.00 Air Mail
Florida Addressees Add 6% Sales Tax.

MILITARY PURCHASE ORDERS ACCEPTED
GOV'T I.M.P.A.C. ACCEPTED

PRICES SUBJECT TO CHANGE